O

A Sequel

Joey Salazar

Dedications

Thank you, to those who have supported me in my writings. It's flattering that I have a small fan base, but it means the world to me each time my book is read. As a special thanks, I want to say thank you to K. P. Taylor, an old billiards mentor of mine who has helped me get through some very frustrating thoughts and moments in life. It was with this gentlemen that I finished my second book after months of writers block! The escape and experience he gave me seriously helped to clear my head. I also want to thank Ms. Karin Hart Swelling for going through both my books and correcting a lot of my bad grammar… as well as my lack of commas. Also, I want to thank someone very special to me, without her I would have never even begun to write this series.

I only hope that she reads it until the end.

It'll be a surprising twist nobody will forget!

Aeternum et Semper

Chapter One

Some people come into your life for a brief moment in time altering your course of life, although some people stay in your life to share your world. The thugs scattered throughout the alleyway lured by Jason came in so he may test his abilities, but in no way did they alter his path. Each one of them lies motionless. The rain falls slowly on Jason, each lightning strike revealing the blood dripping from the clenched knuckles he holds beside him. Jason's face rests emotionless with no sign of remorse or guilt for what he's done to the unsuspecting hoodlums. The thugs initiated the fight, yes, but Jason knew exactly what he was doing; baiting them as a fisherman does trout.

Jason dressed in lavished clothing and showing off a few hundred dollar bills knowing the greed of human nature would kick in tempting the men into desire. He played these men like a fiddle, snapping the strings with every blow to their bodies; orchestrating a well tuned fight, although he expected receive not a single any injury, he did however, come into contact with one of the crooks edge of a blade.

"Damn it, I need to get stronger if I'm going to rely on my own strength," Jason says.

You can use me for your training, Jack responds from within, *even though you're using the adrenaline, it will help you to increase your own strength by lifting heavier weights than you're used to.*

"No, I must do this on my own," Jason whispers. The thugs remain spread out as Jason walks away, hands full of blood. The rain helps to wash the scarlet liquid away from him, but the result is a trail marking his path.

Jason has been training his body with weight lifting techniques, various martial arts, and rigorous conditioning against pain. All his efforts focused on not having to rely on Jack and his superhuman strength. He's determined to keep who he is in tact and not let Jack's and his own psyche merge together like Sabrina has warned him many times. Often Jason will go out and pick fights with people at bars, parks, or wherever he may find an ill-tempered person. Sometimes he'll even put himself out as a naive rich kid just waiting to be robbed. Through this routine Jason's body has become scarred, mostly from his fights early on.

He's studied many different art forms of the martial combat so he knows how to protect himself when needed as well as end a fight quickly if need be. Jason trains alone without a sparring partner primarily due to the fact that he's deserted all but one of his friends in fear any one of them may learn his buried secret. If he ever lost control and allowed himself to take on the adrenaline, Jason would have the strength to rip a car clean in half if he wanted, but doesn't wish to use this strength since doing so too many times could have dire repercussions such as hurting someone indirectly.

After about a forty minute run Jason finally arrives back at Sabrina's mansion in the forest near town. He doesn't bother with opening the gates, but rather he elegantly treks up a tall tree, darting his way from branch to branch over the twelve-foot fence. Landing smoothly as a cat on his feet, knees bent as a cat would, Jason rises from the impact-absorbing stance and continues on his way to the front door.

"Jason!? Is that you?" Sabrina calls out when she hears the entrance doors creak open.

"Yeah, it's me, Sabrina, I'm back from town," Jason calls out closing the large, wooden doors behind him. Sabrina rushes down the metal spiral staircase and straight to Jason as he throws his leather jacket onto a coat rack bolted behind the door. She stops as soon as her eyes capture his image. Clothes ripped, torn and dyed in the scarlet color that screams out his transgressions. Sabrina doesn't think about whose blood it may be, she only springs to his side without a second thought taking his arm with an iron grip leading him down to the basement and into her personal infirmary.

"Jason, you can't keep doing this. It's not safe for you!" She scolds with every step down the spiral stairs. "What if you end up running into the wrong person and they kill you!?" Jason stays silent with only a sigh in response.

Jason is lead over to the medicine table taking a seat on the uncomfortable green bed. "Take off your shirt so I can examine the extent of your injuries," Sabrina orders. Jason does so obediently. He slowly and carefully lifts up his shirt revealing scars scattered up and down his torso ranging from his lower abs climbing up to the base of his neck. The multitude of scars vary in depth, some deep, others merely scratches and are very much spread apart. The current wound Jason's received is a slash just under his left pectoral with about a three inch span leaving Sabrina with grief and fear while her imagination runs wild with thoughts of what could've happened to him. The color in her eyes fade as she thinks of how badly the fight might've been.

"You should see the other guy." Jason says noticing the fear in her eyes hoping to lighten the tension filling the room. Sabrina's ears are deaf to him with clouds of fear covering her. He takes note of this as he notices her body shaking as though she were sitting bare in the arctic. Jason takes Sabrina's trembling hand within his own and in a calm, low voice he tries to relieve her spirit. "Sabrina, stop trembling, I'm alive without severe injuries."

Red emerges around her pupils as she slaps Jason across the face with her free hand. "That doesn't matter! You had me worried! I didn't know if you were coming back this time!" Sabrina yells out; the redness from her eyes increasing, producing tears trickling down the sides of her cheeks. She lowers her head trying to hide her eyes from him, but Jason places two fingers under the tip of her chin slowly raising her head back up and with the same hand he clears the tears from her eyes.

"Sabrina, I'm sorry, but you know how important this is to me. I have to get stronger. Who knows what we'll have to face in the future."

"I know! I just get so worried," Sabrina says looking into Jason's eyes "I'm sorry for slapping you."

"It's fine, I've felt worse pain," Jason says looking down as his fingers run down the side of his torso, "trust me."

Sabrina places one hand on his chest, just above the slash, feeling his heart beating within his ribs. She lets her body go into auto pilot as her mind slips into a trance, almost thoughtless as she cleans the wound with a wet hand towel. A few moments pass before she collects herself turning to the medical table behind her slapping on a couple of medical gloves. Gloves on tightly, Sabrina fills a small syringe with anesthesia then proceeds to takes up a roll of surgical suture while picking out a proper needle.

"Do you want to test out the sealing technique again later?" Jason asks as Sabrina turns around with the syringe in her hand.

"You know we can test it all we want, but I won't know for sure if it works until I'm able to use it on L," She says sliding the needle into Jason's chest injecting him with the anesthetic.

Jason's left eye winces from the sting of the needle. "Yeah, I know, but we'll only have one shot at it!" He says as his eye returns to normal, "I don't want to screw this up."

"We won't, Jason. All you have to do is restrain her and then I'll be able to have as much time as I need to seal her persona away." Sabrina removes the syringe from his chest taking the needle and surgical suture threading it properly. She places one hand on Jason's small firm chest, as if to hold him still, inserting the needle where the slash begins. Jason flinches slightly. She retracts her hand swiftly "I'm sorry, I didn't give the anesthetics enough time to take effect."

Jason grabs her wrist firmly stopping its retreat. "No, keep going, my body needs to get used to pain anyway."

"But this pain is…"

"Any kind of pain; I need to become calloused if I want to survive without relying on Jack."

"I understand," Sabrina says sticking the needle back in. She concentrates intently on sewing up the wound without any further exchange of words between them.

Do you think Jason will be able to confront L? Shae asks from within Sabrina's head.

What do you mean? Sabrina asks with only her thoughts.

Jason and L were together for quite some time. He may still have feelings for her.

Jason knows that his feelings for her weren't real, he knows they were just the result of her abilities. Sabrina thinks within her mind.

Sabrina, whether his feelings were artificial or not, they were there.

Sabrina stops sewing. Contemplating Shae's thoughts, her face falls back into a blank trance of racing thoughts. She thinks that Jason may be the reason why the plan could fail. She wonders if he'll fall back under her influence and become her heart throbbing slave again.

"Why did you stop?" Jason asks.

"Jason, I think we'll have to work on another technique before we actually confront L," Sabrina says keeping her eyes locked on his wound.

"What would that be?" he asks.

"Let me finish and then I'll explain. I need to focus."

Jason smirks.

Sabrina stitches up the last portion of the slash in his chest applying ointment and gauze over the wound. "Your body is going to need time to heal. Refrain from any training for at least a few days." Jason just smirks again. "I'm serious, Jason! You can't have that wound open up again. It's really deep!"

"I'll lay off it for today, but I'm going to resume my training first thing in the morning," he says getting up from the table allowing the light to showcase his abdomens and chest. Sabrina, entranced by the gallery of muscles, loses control of her eyes; tracing his torso up and down admiring his slenderness, the jagged abs, the ripe obliques, and his small but firm chest. Her vision glazes over with desire but she knows she must refrain. The two haven't ventured in that area of unknown ambiguity.

"Weren't you going to tell me about some other technique you need to work on?" Jason asks snapping Sabrina back to reality.

"Oh," flustered, she tries recollecting her thoughts, "yeah, it's about L."

"What about her?"

"Well, her ability. She can manipulate the chemicals inside someone," Sabrina explains, "raising the Oxytocin levels causing someone to basically become a slave in love with her and willing to do whatever she wishes."

"Yeah?" Jason says hiding his sculpted body underneath a clean v-neck shirt unsullied with blood. "So?"

"So…" Sabrina starts hesitantly.

Go on Sabrina, just tell him Shae urges from within.

I'm sure he'll get upset that I would even suggest it, Sabrina replies in thought.

Regardless, get on with it, Shae says with sternness inside Sabrina's mind.

"What if L tries to use her ability on you again?"

"What?" Jason asks seemingly oblivious.

"I mean, let's say you do confront L again, how do you know you won't fall back under her spell?" Sabrina asks with fear in her voice. "How do you know you'll be mentally strong enough to resist her?"

"That's ridiculous!" Jason shouts in anger, "How could you even think that!?" Jason turns, walking toward the stairs. "Do you know how much I despise her for what she did!? You think I'm that weak?" he takes hold of the railing spiraling upwards patiently waiting for a response.

"It's not that I think you're weak," she begins carefully "it's just you were with her for two years." Sabrina lowers her head with jealousy from the thought of it. "She knows you inside and out. I'm sure she can easily get to you again."

"I can't believe you would think I'd still be vulnerable for that wretch." Jason says in a low angered voice disappearing up the stairs.

"I told you he would get upset," Sabrina speaks into the empty room with her head still hung.

He shouldn't have been so upset, Shae says from within again.

"Whatever!" Sabrina shouts springing her head back up "him getting so upset over me saying anything just proves that he still feels something for her and I'm not just talking about the distain he speaks of."

Jason slips into a dark, leather jacket from his closet then proceeds to the nearby window in his room opening it up to the wind and rain storming outside.

"Psh, how could she think I could be so weak?" He says hoping onto the window seal.

She has a point though, Jack says manifesting into an ethereal form beside him.

"Don't tell me you think I'm weak, too!"

I'm just saying, Jack replies *She has a point.*

"Both of you need to just get off my back!" Jason says aloud jumping out of the second story window landing softly with bent knees as to absorb the impact on the grass below.

Are you just going to leave the window open? Jack says remaining inside. Jason rises to his feet taking a look up to where his ethereal form is. Without a word, he turns and walks off into the storm. *I guess not* Jack dissipates into the wind and rain remaining tethered to Jason.

Sabrina, still down in the infirmary cleaning up the mess on her operating table, can't help but hope that Jason doesn't have feelings for L still other than those he speaks of. Wrapping up the surgical suture, she tosses the bloody hand towels into a near by hamper, and sanitizes the needle placing it back on her table of surgical tools.

"Damn that Jason. He should know that I'm only thinking about his safety," Sabrina slams her fist on the green bed. "He's so stubborn!" Her fist shaking, drops of tears land nearby dancing around her clenched hand. Her voice emits a whispering sob as she tries to swallow her sadness.

"You know what!?" She exclaims straightening into a full upright posture, "I'm going to give that jerk a piece of my mind!"

Is that wise, Sabrina? Shae asks.

"I don't care! He didn't have to get so mad!" Sabrina blurts out as Shae just lets out a sigh.

Sabrina rushes up the staircase to the second floor darting in a beeline fashion to Jason's room. Without a second thought she busts into his room. "Jason! You can't just…" but stops short, noticing the vacancy. She looks over to the open window and slowly walks over. "Damn it," Sabrina whispers as she slowly closes the window.

Jason walks the streets of downtown trying to shake off his anger in the slowly falling rain. He takes in the scenery, noticing lights of flickering at the Library Bar and Grill where he had his first real formal meeting with Sabrina. "Damn, I can't believe it's already been six months," he says pulling out a cigarette and placing it between his lips.

I thought you quit? Jack asks

"Yeah, well, old habits die hard."

Thus Sabrina's reasoning for what she said Jack says in direct correlation.

"Whatever," Jason lights the cigarette taking the path of the adjacent alleyway. He takes a couple of puffs and tries to let out the stress with exhaled smoke.

Jason is slowly covered in a coat of liquid while the rain slowly falls over the city. Out of nowhere lightening strikes!

Jason, takes a split second to get out the way, saving his hide, abandons his cigarette as it falls to the floor splitting in two.

"What the hell was that!?" Jason yells out in shock. Without warning a second strike of lightening comes down, and yet again with Jason's keen reflexes, manages to evade the stream of electricity. "What the hell is going on here!?"

"Well, I obviously underestimated you," an unknown voice says from atop a fire escape. Jason looks up, but the darkened alleyway casts a shadow over his face.

"Who are you!?" Jason yells out, but the silhouetted figure remains silent as another bolt of lightening strikes down upon Jason, barely grazing his torso causing his previous wound to open up again. Jason falls to one knee taking hold of his abdomen as the blood begins to flow through his fingers. He looks up at him again "you're doing this, aren't you!?"

The silhouette sends one more shock to the wall next to Jason, intentionally missing as if answering Jason's question with action rather than words.

Damn it, who is this guy? Jason thinks to himself.

The man jumps down from the fire escape. Little shreds of electricity spark between the bottom of his shoes and the floor he lands on. It appears that the energy current allows him lightly hover above the floor instead of just falling. The assailant's landing is so well executed keeping a shadow just over his face as to remain hidden.

"Your L's ex-boyfriend, are you not?" The man asks.

Jason's eyes widen with surprise. "How do you know L!? Who are the hell are you?"

"Just call me O," the man says. "But you don't need to remember it as I'll be painting the walls with your blood!" O shouts as another bolt of lightening rages down from the sky toward Jason.

Chapter Two

"That stupid Jason," Sabrina says looking through the window. She turns around stomping her way out of his room when she notices his phone sitting on the nightstand next to his bed. "Of course, leave your phone so I can't even call you, how typical of him!" She closes his door behind her as she exits his room and mumbles in frustration "I don't get why he has to get so bent out of shape whenever L's brought up."

Sabrina, Shae replies, *understand that she betrayed him. He fell in love with this girl only to find out the truth about her.*

"But it wasn't real."

It was for him, Shae answers.

The Sinclair family has been in business for the last sixty-three years owning a chain of laboratories spanning throughout the United States. Sinclair Industries, the company her grandfather built, deals with much scientific experimentation and technological development such as human behavioral studies, evolutionary adaptations, biological cybernetics, and other such fields with the goal of expanding human capabilities. Sabrina was being trained by her parents to run the company in hopes of her taking over the family business.

She had private teachers coupled with intensive private course schedules outside of a social learning environment. With the lack of a social schooling institute Sabrina lacked the opportunity to connect with any other peers with the exception of her tutors. All of her training and schooling took most of her time leaving her no room for a social life, although it would all be worth it with the company being taken over someday, but the Sinclair Corporation was inherited sooner than Sabrina expected.

Jason, having saved Sabrina's life, has spent the last six months living in her family's mansion. He was given a room of his own on the second floor of the mansion where he moved in his stuff shortly after learning of Sabrina's own abilities of telepathy. In those six months, Sabrina and Jason talked over the possibilities of what they could do with their own powers and abilities. The two talked over the pros and cons regarding misuse, the higher opportunities they had above others, and also the dangers their abilities posed.

In their discussions, they often brought L up and her own powers. She's able to manipulate the chemicals in someone else's biological system causing the individual to feel any emotion she wants. Whether it's happiness, sadness, anger, hate, or even love, L has complete control over anyone's emotions, which in turn could be very dangerous. Sabrina has seen what she did to Jason and has convinced Jason that L cannot be allowed to toy with people. He reluctantly agreed with Sabrina and realized that the two had to stop L and strip her of her powers, which would not be so easy. Just as Jason was placed under her spell, so to would others be. So in those six months Jason has been preparing his body and mind while he and Sabrina searched for her, although it's proven unfruitful thus far.

Without touching the door to Jason's room, Sabrina slams it shut using only her mind. *You've perfected your Mind Barrier technique very well, Sabrina,* Shae compliments in regard to Sabrina's display of her telekinesis.

"Thank you, Shae, with the Mind Barrier technique I can use your powers all I want without having to fuse our persona's together!" Sabrina makes her way to the stair case banister that overlooks the front door to her mansion. The banister to their staircase is quite uniquely made with jet-black railings that spiral across the posts, reaching to the base and branching across the floor like roots which seamlessly meld with the bleak, onyx wooden floors.

"I'm still working my other techniques as well," she says as she throws herself over the banister, "like my Floating technique." Sabrina reaches the onyx colored floor but stops short of her bare feet touching the cold surface hovering just inches off the ground for only a few seconds before gently returning to the earth. Sabrina smiles widely letting out a small giggle.

Sabrina, don't be so modest. You've come a long way with perfecting your abilities! Shae compliments once again.

"It takes so much concentration to use my abilities without combining with you and even more attentiveness when focusing on actions like levitating myself. I'm sure I could do so much more than these parlor tricks."

But you're abilities have been increasing every day! You haven't had to make us fuse together since that horrible car accident on the highway half a year ago.

"Yeah, and if it wasn't for Jason, I'm sure I would have died that night!" Sabrina exclaims with an even larger smile growing.

Let's be honest, that night when our persona's blended together, we were able to erect a barrier around your body and that's what saved you. Shae explains.

"Yeah, that's true, too, but it wasn't strong enough!" Sabrina stomps her foot with her arm extending toward an ethereal form one finger pointed at Shae appearing before her. "The barrier didn't last very long, nor was it made through skill. The barrier was just a reflex, and even so I passed out there in the driver seat!" Shae crosses her ghastly arms as Sabrina continues. "plus my car exploded!"

Yeah, well, I guess you're right, Shae says dropping her arms and raising them out toward Sabrina as if to hug her. *Either way, your abilities have increased so much since then!*

"Thank you, Shae!" Sabrina exclaims moving forward for a hug, although they pass right through each other. Sabrina tilts her head backwards letting out a small giggle, "oh yeah, I forget you're just a projection of my mind, he-he!" Sabrina follows her gaze and twirls around with her black skirt following in the same fashion. She concentrates for a moment and soon her feet rise three inches off the ground levitating herself through the hallway into the kitchen and straight to the fridge setting herself on the cold tile floor.

"Eek!" Sabrina shrieks out from the freezing floor beneath her feet and immediately shoots herself off the ground straight into the ceiling. Her head crashes hard sending her back down flipping up her skirt as she falls on her butt. The pain from falling is more apparent than the coldness of the floor so she just sits there rubbing her head.

"Ouch, that really hurt."

Sabrina, that was amazing! Shae says looking down at her.

"Amazing!?" Sabrina picks herself up off the floor returning to her feet. "Hitting my head was amazing?"

No, you usually can only levitate yourself off the floor a few inches, but this time you rose all the way to ceiling!

"Hey, yeah, you're right!" Sabrina comes to the realization of her sudden progress rising off the floor once more. "I am getting better!" Filled with happiness, she twirls around in circles just inches off the floor, and, as her emotions rise, so does her power in her abilities. The kitchen cabinets begin to flap, the utensils around the kitchen start swirling around, and the food in pantry suddenly flies out joining the utensils in their vortex orbiting around her. Sabrina doesn't notice what's taking place around her she continues to twirl and twirl like a feather dancing in the wind.

Sabrina! Calm down! Shae calls out. *Open your eyes!* Sabrina stops mid air and opens her eyes to see everything in the vortex suddenly stop just as she did. Shocked by the disaster in the kitchen, her feet once again meet the tile floor and everything else falls to the ground as well with a great crashing noise.

"Did I, uhh, do all this?" She asks looking over at Shae next to her.

It seems your powers were heightened by your emotions, Shae begins. *I guess you need to focus on more than just trying to use your powers and feel them within yourself.*

"Oh, awesome! I really could only levitate one thing at a time, but everything in the kitchen!?" Sabrina begins picking things up off the floor one by one. "This is incredible!"

Sabrina, why don't you try putting everything away using only telekinesis? Sabrina looks up at Shae's ethereal form blank faced pondering the idea.

"That's a great idea!" She drops the items back to floor as she rises to her feet. "I could make a mess of everything in the kitchen, so why not clean everything up at once!" She takes a few steps back so she can see everything in plain view. Looking at a loaf of bread, Sabrina manipulates her powers and raises it off the floor. She turns her concentration to a nearby spatula and starts to lift it off the ground as well, but the loaf of bread falls back to the floor.

"What the heck?" She tilts her head slightly to the side in confusion. "Why isn't it working?"

Try concentrating a bit harder, Shae advises. Taking her advice, Sabrina tries once more, but this time she's able to lift both the bread and spatula together. Although she's succeeded, they both fall to floor once more.

"Damn it. C'mon, stupid powers!"

Maybe use your hands to channel your powers?

Sabrina squints her eyes holding her left hand out and placing two fingers to the side of her head hoping to use her hands as a medium to focus her concentration. Directing her left hand toward the two objects, they begin to rise off the ground flawlessly. With a wave of her hand, both items levitate their way over to the granite counter top and are placed down gently.

"Shae, did you see that!? It worked!" Sabrina exclaims with excitement.

Good job, Sabrina, at this rate you're going to have your abilities mastered in no time!

Sabrina then extends both her hands in the direction of the mess. "Watch this!" Her hands turn inward so her palms are facing one another while her fingers spread apart. With her hands, she makes an imaginary sphere between her hands and closes her eyes. Within in a few seconds everything in the kitchen rises once more. Sabrina opens her eyes and begins tapping her fingers on her imaginary sphere as each item flies across the rooms to its own respective place. The food is placed back in her storage closet, the utensils return to the drawers from which they came, and all the cabinets close one by one.

Shae's eyes widen as she witnesses the power Sabrina is able to give off. Shae is amazed by Sabrina's control over her abilities, although, she notices herself fading.

What? What's going on? Shae looks down at her hands as they begin to fade away. *The barrier must be collapsing within her.* Shae looks back up at Sabrina. *Sabrina, stop, we're starting combine again!* Shae's words fall on deaf ears. Sabrina seems too wrapped up in the power she's demonstrating.

She's giving too much of her concentration toward manipulating the items before her that she isn't keeping the barrier in mind that she's set between Shae's persona and her own. The fusion of the two personas's increases little by little every second the barrier decreases in power.

In order for Sabrina to use her abilities, her persona and Shae's persona would need to fuse together each time. Sabrina was able to use her telepathic abilities when she was fused with Shae before to erect a barrier between their two persona's while maintaining her granted powers, but this takes concentration, not much, but without her focusing on the barrier at all, there would be nothing stopping the fusion of the personas.

Dropping her hands down, Sabrina finishes putting everything away in the kitchen with her telekinesis ability. "Shae, did you see that? I was able to control everything in the…" but Sabrina stops the moment she notices how faded Shae's ethereal form is. "Shae? What's up with you?" Immediately she notices the barrier within her mind is fading and quickly focuses her mental abilities back toward the barrier and in no time, it's raised right back up.

You need to be more careful, Sabrina. Shae's voice slowly travels from inside Sabrina's head and back to the ethereal form increasing in visibility.

"I'm sorry, Shae, I guess I just got a little carried away."

Try not to use too much power at once or the barrier between us won't sustain, Shae advises looking down at her hands as she retains her full visibility.

"Yeah, definitely!" Sabrina's stomach lets out a faint growl of hunger.

Now why don't you try making dinner, hmmm?

"Ha-ha, that would be a good idea, wouldn't it?" Agreeing, Sabrina rubs the back of her head in embarrassment. She turns back to the refrigerator swinging the door wide open and begins her search of food. "Hmmm... What to cook?" Raising one finger to the bottom of her chin she thinks about Jason. "What do you think Jason would want?"

Jason likes pizza, but you don't have the ingredients to make one.

"What about spaghetti and meatballs?"

Jason left without even saying goodbye, and you're going to cook him dinner?

"Yeah, why not?" Sabrina asks turning around. "Sure he still gets upset whenever She is brought up, but that shouldn't bother me. It's not like he likes me anyway. We're just... just..."

Just what?

"We're just friends trying to stop Her. She can't be allowed to control people the way She does, and we both mutually feel that way, that's all."

If you ask me, I think you're being stupid about it, Shae says as her ethereal form dissipates in the air.

"Whatever, just dissipate like you always do whenever we disagree!" Sabrina growls into the empty air whipping herself back toward the stainless steel refrigerator. "Spaghetti and meatballs it is!"

Sabrina causes a small pound of meat to hover it's way out of the freezer unwrapping itself on the way toward her. As the meat reaches her, a bowl finds it's way through the air and scoops the meat up making it's way over to the microwave. Sabrina opens the microwave door as a gentleman would do for his lady, and let's the bowl slide right in closing the door behind it. She sets it for defrost and turns her attention toward the pantry storage closet. Bringing out the spaghetti, she simultaneously levitates a pot out of a nearby cabinet and has it set on the stove for her. She grabs hold of the spaghetti tearing the bag open with her hands and emptying the contents into the pot.

"Wow! I AM getting better at this!" She says as she smiles from ear to ear. "Now let's try something tricky!" Using her telekinesis powers again, she turns the sink's water faucet on letting the water pour out. She concentrates on the water, but doesn't entirely succeed in raising the amount she wants. Holding out both her hands, she creates a bowl in the form of her hands and suddenly the water begins to gather itself together in the same shape she is creating in her hands. "Nice!"

Sabrina begins to expand her hands keeping both hands in the same shape making it possible for her to gather even more water together beneath the faucet. When she finally collects enough together, she flicks her head down and shuts off the water faucet. Carefully guiding her hands sideways in the direction of the pot, the collected water follows as if her hands are extended beneath. Getting the water over the pot, she turns both her hands parallel to one another and in doing so, the water begins to pour out of itself and into the pot of spaghetti sticks.. "Yes! I did it!"

Sabrina walks over to the stove, turning on the heat so the water may begin to boil. Some time later, the microwave beeps with sounds of completion. Sabrina removes the bowl placing it next to the stovetop and proceeds with bringing out a pan and placing it on the stove as well. She takes a few steps back as she raises the defrosted meat into he air. Shooting out both her hands int the direction of the meat, she begins to split the meat into separate pieces and each rolls into small circular balls as her hands orchestrate the means to do so. Each meatball is then set into the pan one by one, and she turns the heat on so they may cook.

"Now why didn't I think to cook like this all the time?" She says to herself feeling very accomplished. "Too bad Jason couldn't see me in action." Sabrina shakes her head flinging the idea out of her mind. "No, can't think about it. Just keep cooking, Sabrina!" She says to herself as she walks over to a nearby drawer. She pulls out a stirring spoon and walks back over to the stove. She then begins to stir the spaghetti in as the water continues to boil and move around the meatballs so they can cook on each side evenly.

Sabrina scoops the spaghetti into separate plates and hovers the meat balls onto each plate as well. She equips both plates with a single fork each and walks the plates over to the dinner table. "He likes Coca-Cola. Right," she says bringing out two cans of the product over to the table using nothing but a couple of fingers levitating them in the air straight onto the table next to the two plates.

"Right! The table is set," Sabrina says feeling proud of the meal she's prepared with her abilities. "Now, I've just got to wait for Jason to come back home." Sabrina looks down at her phone noticing about an hour has passed since he's left. "He shouldn't be gone too long, maybe I'll paint while I wait."

From the kitchen, through the dining room and down a nearby hallway lies Sabrina's study. In here she keeps her library; hundreds of books ranging from fictional entertainment to knowledge filled pages. Here is her easel, pastel tools and her escape. Sabrina reaches slowly for her black pastel crayon and yet stops midway. She retracts her hand back toward her side and without another movement, the same pastel floats elegantly into the air. The pastel traces it's way across the canvas as two more pastels rise. A blue and gray utensil float onto the white paper and simultaneously dance across the page with the black.

Her eyes close, she stands motionless and allows her mind to work through the pastels in creating a depiction in her mental state. The pastels move faster as three more pages rise into the air. More pastels defy gravity snapping to the hovering pages. Two pages at each of her side and one behind her, she's surrounded as if four walls of blank canvases box her into an unseen room of her own mind's creation.

Sabrina's eyes remain shut and the pastels dance across each page surrounding her of their own accord. The strokes become quicker, the lines much finer and the picture grows more and more vibrantly vivid with each passing moment. Each picture drawn seems only to be a piece of a puzzle. The portraits show only a glimpse of her mind's true image. Even so, the blank canvases are littered with color and images soon becoming something of a masterpiece in their own right.

Sabrina opens her eyes looking at the picture before her. A giant, bright blue streak treads from the top of the page down to the bottom. Only the right of the page shows the blue streak while the other half shows the sky, stars and tops of buildings behind them. The drawing to her right is like an exact mirror image of the first with the same blue streak and setting. The other two drawings placed side by side show the back of someone. The hair of the drawn character is darkly black, his appearance seems to be drenched and wet with water and his shirt outlines what seem to be bandages underneath. As these two drawing have come together, the other two levitate above as all four delineate one single picture. Realizing what the pictures show, Sabrina gasps, "Jason?"

Chapter Three

Jason made a quick dash forward just barely dodging the bolt of lightning cast down by O. Keeping momentum he sprang toward the man, fist clenched and cocked, ready to make contact, but before he could make contact with his hidden face a shockwave disbursed from O casts Jason to the flat of his back.

"It's useless, there's no way you could beat me, Jason," O said as electricity sparked on the tips of his fingers. "I control electricity! NOW DIE!" O pointed a single finger in Jason's direction and like a gun, he shot out small orbs of electricity. Jason rolled backward managing to escape the orbs; pushed up with his hands planted on the ground and sprang back up to his feet. As soon as he found his footing a small orb impacted his chest, and he was once again knocked back to the floor.

Jason, you can't beat this guy by yourself. You need me, Jack, Jason's persona, said inside his head. Ignoring Jack's words he raised back up to his feet once again.

"You have a death wish, don't you?" O said lowering his finger. Jason didn't respond. "Let's see how you like this!" O brought both his hands together forming a semi-circle, generating electricity within, creating a sphere of surging energy. The glow it was emitting shed some light on O's appearance. His face seemed to have a slight tan, and an eerie smile that reached from ear to ear. He was enjoying this; Jason could see it in his maniacal smile. As he spoke, his defined and chiseled chin moved awkwardly, as though it was having fits of spasms. Jason couldn't quite make out his hair color or style since it was sheltered with some kind of reflective hood. *Why would his hood shine like that?* Jason thought to himself.

O let the ball of energy free causing it to accelerate quickly toward Jason. *It's coming at me too fast!* Jason thought in fear, *I won't be able to dodge this!* At the same time, Jack interrupted *Damn it, Jason! I can't let you die!* Suddenly Jason could feel his brain being overwhelmed. Jason and Jack's persona's fused together sending waves of adrenaline racing in his veins. Jason used his new strength in his legs to leap ten feet into the air allowing the ball of energy to pass right under his feet. The ball of energy crashed into a nearby dumpster behind him. As Jason landed back on his feet, he noticed the dumpster had created a hole in the wall.

What if I was hit by that blast? he thought to himself. *I would have been a goner.* Jason turns his attention back to O, *this guy is no joke. He intends to end my life. But why is L putting him up to this?*

"I can tell you're petrified with fear of my power," O began "so why don't you just surrender since you know you cannot win?"

"That's a joke right?" Jason smirked "You really think I would let myself lose to some cocky idiot like you?"

"How dare you disrespect me!" O yells out. Lights of electricity sparked beneath his feet and erected a small shockwave springing him toward Jason with great speed. His right hand, raging with sparks, created a blade of energy and reached out toward Jason. It was as though his hand had become a dagger made of pure electricity.

With his heightened reflexes, Jason made a quick step to the side dodging the edge of his O's fingertips. As he did, Jason reached out his right hand grabbing O by the neck stopping him in his tracks. His hand squeezed O's neck with great force causing O's eyes to turn blood shot red from the pressure.

"Jason! Stop!" Jack shouted out loud with his and Jason's voice sounding fused together out loud. "It's kill or be killed!" Jason responded with the same voice. O, realizing what was going on within Jason, saw his opportunity and thrust his spark equipped hand through Jason's left shoulder. Jason's grip loosened around O's neck from the pain, and quickly cast O to the side slamming him into the brick wall of the alleyway. Jason immediately used his strength to bound between fire escapes to make his escape. Jason ran off leaving O lying unconscious as the clouds dissipated.

With Jason still fused with Jack, he uses his strength to leap from rooftop to rooftop, distancing himself from the alleyway as much as he can. The buildings vary in size being either two story, three story or even four story buildings. With his tremendous strength, he's able to take each landing without pain and leap to the top of any building in a single bound. The strength Jack provides Jason is incredible. He is also able to pick up great speeds with the power in legs. Jason has been able to run a single mile in less than two minutes. His strength is unparalleled.

Alright Jack, Jason says as he's put fifteen blocks between himself and O, *let's split now.* Jason's persona separates from Jack allowing him to take full control. Jason feels the adrenaline coursing through his body slow, it's flowing pace and his strength returning to normal. The pain in his chest from O's electrical blade grows more apparent as the blood begins to seep out of the wound. He takes hold of his wound right away but with such a huge gash in his shoulder, the blood keeps flowing out despite the pressure applied.

Jason, we should stay mentally fused together, Jack advises within, *the adrenaline your body provides can help slow the bleeding!*

"No, we can't keep combining our personas," Jason falls to his knees in pain, placing his free hand on the concrete of the building roof, "I can't let us.."

The loss of so much blood suffocates his brain sending his vision into a blur and fatiguing his body to the point of trembling. Jason tries getting back up to his feet and walks inches at a time.

You need me, Jason!

"I can't.." Jason's speech slows up as his consciousness begins to fade. With every inch he gets closer and closer to the edge of the rooftop.

"We can't … fuse…" Placing his hand on the ledge of the rooftop, Jason attempts to look over trying to find the fire escape leading down to the sidewalk. As he leans over the side of the building blood continues to pour out of his body at an alarming rate.

"Without… Sabrina," His voice fades, eyes slowly close, and his body's trembling stops in a limp, dead weight fashion. Leaned over the edge, his body succumbs to the laws of gravity falling toward the ground from atop the four story building.

Jason knew he would have to fight one of L's pawns sooner or later. He trained for the confrontation, he was vigorously preparing himself for that battle, but he just didn't know what to expect. Sabrina warned him that the others had powers too, but controlling electricity was not even a possibility within his mind. It's obvious now that with all of Jason's training, he's still not strong enough to take on L and whoever she has backing her.

After learning of L's deceit, he vowed to himself that he would stop her. He would keep her from controlling anyone else with her chemical manipulating abilities. Sabrina felt for

Jason because of what L did to him and also felt indebted for having her life saved by him as well. About a week after Good Friday, Sabrina invited Jason to come live with her inside her mansion. With her parents gone, and her brother in Pittsburgh, she was living inside her eight-thousand square foot home by herself with no one to keep her company except her two pets and a pair of housekeepers. She didn't know him very well, but with the thought of him saving her life, she knew he couldn't be a bad person, plus she had to repay him somehow.

After some time of living together Jason asked Sabrina if she would help him stop L from abusing her powers. He thought of the mental wall Sabrina is able to erect between herself and Shae which got him thinking that, if she honed her skills, she could seal someone's powers for good. That's when Jason started training himself. He knew that if they were going to go up against L and her puppets that he would need to rely on more than just his powers, hopefully not having to use them at all. Although he trained very hard, he still wasn't ready for the fight with O.

The lights are bright, blinding and relentless. Jason raises his right arm to shield his face from the overpowering light blinking a couple of times trying to habituate his vision to the atmosphere. He tries raising his body from the flat of his back but is denied by the pain in his shoulder. Jason pulls his arm down and reaches over to his left shoulder hoping to ease the pain. He takes hold of his wound, but much to his surprise he doesn't feel flesh or blood but a bandage over the deep gash.

"What the hell?" Jason grunts as the lights dim and turn away revealing Sabrina standing over him.

"How are you feeling?" Sabrina asks bringing a glass of water with a straw to his mouth. Jason takes a sip and a deep breath, closing his eyes. "I found you falling from a building covered in blood. What happened to you!?"

"I was attacked by one of L's lackeys," Jason says taking another sip of water. "He's able to control electricity."

Sabrina's eyes widen hearing the shocking news. "So there are more out there like us. What did you find out from him?"

"He didn't say much, but he knows who I am and was bent on killing me."

"Obviously. He left a hole in your chest dislocating your shoulder." She says as she runs her fingers through his light reflecting black hair.

"How did you get me? What happened?" Jason asks brushing Sabrina's hand aside as he pushed through the pain bringing himself to a sitting position.

"Like I said, I found you falling from a rooftop," Sabrina's voice loses it's sympathetic tone.

"But how did you know where to find me?"

Sabrina recalls the painting she made and debated if she should tell him how her powers seemed to increase with thoughts of him. "I just sensed that you were in trouble." She concluded to keep it to herself. "I took the Jeep and just followed my gut feeling."

"And what? You caught me?" Jason asks tracing his eyes up and down her slender body.

"Not physically. I was able to keep you from hitting the ground with my abilities."

"Really!?" Jason's eyes snapped up to look her in the face with shock. "How were you able to.. I didn't know you had that much control!"

"You have no idea," Sabrina says pulling her hair back from her face.

Jason silently lowers his head as his eyes gaze down at his bandages. He places his hand over his shoulder gently, squinting from the pain, as he gauges his strength. "Sabrina, I'm not ready for this."

"We knew this would be hard, Jason, but look what she's done. She uses others to get to you."

"But why? Why now?" Jason gets off the familiar green table. "It's been six months since I last spoke to her."

"Maybe she feels threatened from what you told her last time?" Sabrina hands Jason a clean shirt. "She probably hasn't been able to do anything since then."

Jason slips into the shirt and makes his way toward the spiral staircase "It doesn't matter, but let's go back and question him."

"We'll go in the morning, Jason. You need your rest," Sabrina says inching closer to him. "Besides, I made food and it's probably cold by now."

"I don't know how long he'll be knocked out though."

"Doesn't matter. Rest and we'll go tomorrow. That'll be the end of it."

Jason scoffs and heads up the stairs and into the dojo beginning his routine sword training.

"Be sure to grab a plate!" Sabrina yells from the infirmary "I left you a plate on the dinning table!"

He didn't even thank you for helping him, Shae manifests behind Sabrina the moment Jason is out of sight.

"He doesn't have to. I still owe him my life," Sabrina says as she takes off her white coat.

Even after you just saved his and all the previous times you've saved him?

"It's a debt I'll never be able to repay."

Chapter Four

The sun hasn't risen. The moon soon to divorce the sky. Sabrina wakes up rubbing the fatigue from her eyes. The house completely quiet; void of light. She climbs out of bed as her vision adapts to the darkness. She glances down at the clock next to her bed quickly being filled with astonishment. 5:23AM.

"I'm not supposed to wake up for another three hours." Regardless of the time, Sabrina feels a calling to her. Astonishment leaves her body letting curiosity take its place. She closes her eyes opening her mind, trying to sense a disturbance, nothing. Sabrina covers her body in a silk, black nightgown feeling her way through the darkness. The metal knob to her bedroom door is ice cold causing her to pull her hand back quickly. Using her nightgown she twists the nob and opens her creaking door. She flicks a nearby switch illuminating the hall, but nobody is there.

Sabrina stares down the corridor trying to figure out this strange feeling she has inside her. It's as though someone is calling out to her, but she can't seem to hear a single sound except the wind caressing the wooden walls. She slowly follows the lights along the corridor while each step she takes sends chills up her spine. Her bare feet against the cold wooden floor is pleasant and yet unbearably cold. "Did Jason turn the heater off before he went to sleep?" Sabrina wraps her arms around herself trying to shield herself from the heat, but of course this never helped anyone. Halfway down the corridor a light at the end is turned on. "Jason?" Sabrina calls out but no answer. She continues trying to sense something, maybe even his thoughts, but she still can't seem to sense anything.

"Shae, I'm worried," Sabrina says in a very low whisper. *You'll be okay, it's probably just Jason sleep walking or something.* She continues down the hallway with a quickened pace and heightened curiosity coupled with worry. The silence is what worries her the most. Sabrina can usually hear a nearby person's thoughts without even trying, so what could be in her home that doesn't have a single thought.

Sabrina turns the corner of the hallway reaching the staircase banister that overlooks her home's entrance. The door is wide open with the lights on. "What the hell? Did Jason leave?" She jumps over the banister holding her nightgown close to her body as to prevent it from flying up as she falls. Using her telekinetic abilities she allows her bare feet to softly meet the wooden floor. Taking one step at a time Sabrina reaches out for the front door then slowly closing it. Before she can completely close the door a hand reaches in and grabs hold of the side of the door. Sabrina let's out a loud scream and jumps backwards.

Jason's door slams open; Sabrina hears his footsteps racing from upstairs. She jumps backwards and the door swings open, but the darkness outside shields the intruder's face only revealing a neck down view of person in an expensive black suit. Out of nowhere Jason flips over the staircase impacting the ground below quickly dashing in front of Sabrina. "Are you okay!?" He asks looking over his shoulder behind him. She only gives a frightened nod. Jason turns his attention back to the intruder, "Who are you!? What do you want!?"

"Well, I'm glad Sabrina has a guardian in my absence," The man says as he steps into the light. As his face is revealed Sabrina screams out, "Christós!", racing into his arms.

Jason drops his stance in confusion, "You... know this guy?"

"Jason! I'd like you to meet my brother, Christós. He's been away on business since before the accident," Sabrina says smiling from ear to ear as she steps to the side of Christós.

"Well, pajama boy, you know who I am," Christós steps forward reaching his arm out. "Who might you be?"

Jason, wearing nothing but his red pajama pants, not even a shirt to cover up the toned muscles protruding from his upper body, looks down noticing his indecency. He raises his gaze back up to Christós stretching his hand out for a formal handshake, "The name's Jason. Sorry about the acrobatics, Sabrina didn't tell me you were coming."

"I honestly didn't even know," Sabrina says turning her attention back toward Christós. "I thought you were supposed to be in Pittsburgh for another six months brother?"

"I actually moved my work back home to be with you, Sabrina. I just got word about the accident." He walks past Jason placing his coat on a nearby rack "Why didn't you call or send me some kind of message?"

"Well, after the accident, I met Jason here and he's sort of been taking care of me." Her face becomes flushed as the words leave her mouth.

"I see," Christós says turning around to stare into Jason's eyes with intent to kill.

"By 'taking care' she means that in the most platonic way possible!"

"I'm sure she does," Christós smirks. He walks past Jason once more brushing his shoulder on the way. As their shoulders scrape, Jason's back is sent with chills racing down with every hair on his body springing up. Christós takes his bags and makes his way up the wooden stairs. "Sorry for waking the both of you up, but I've had a long flight, and I'll be turning in for the night." He stops at the top of the stairs turning his attention toward Jason and Sabrina before disappearing around the corner, "Oh, and be sure to keep things 'platonic' between the two of you." Both Sabrina and Jason nod their heads and say their goodnights to Christós.

Silence overbears atop Sabrina and Jason as Christós heads to his room. Jason turns to Sabrina slowly, "Your brother's back in town."

"Yeah, it was really unexpected! But I'm happy he's back!"

"He's not going to kill me for staying here, is he?" Jason asks crossing his arms.

"If you don't put a shirt on soon, I think he just might come over with his machete," She says looking down at Jason's chiseled abdomens.

Jason smirks and walks off, "Yeah, well, I'm going to train for a while since I'm awake. You go back to sleep and then, we have to figure out who this O person is."

"Did you get his name at all?" Sabrina asks as Jason turns the corner.

"Just O."

When Jason moved into Sabrina's mansion she had another spare room remade into a dojo for Jason to train in. The room is mirrorless with various weights and weapons for him to train, also equipped with practice dummies and an assortment of wearable weights. With the consequences that come with Jason using his abilities, he knew he needed to gain natural strength and fighting abilities in case he got into any trouble with his goal of taking down L. He knew L had people at her beck and call, but wasn't sure what to expect. Now that he's finally faced one the standard has been set.

Jason enters the dojo and takes hold of his obi wrapping it around his waist then equipping himself with his katana. He slowly walks to the middle of the room setting himself down into a sitting position on his knees placing both hands on the front of his thighs. Eyes closed, breath relaxed, heart decelerates to a slow lifeless beat. In a single second Jason steps up, thrusts his right leg forward and draws his sword making a clean cutting motion forward. Without warning he pushes forward with his other leg bringing him into a forward stance and making a diagonal cut downward shifting the air in the room. As the sword is held toward the ground he closes his eyes once more creating a virtual scenario within his mind. Four enemies, one on each side, each equipped with their own blades and a thirst for blood. He lifts his sword straight out in front of him keeping a forward stance and a focused mind. Jason lifts his eye lids and the scenario manifests around him taking form.

The first enemy behind him quickly advances at him thrusting his sword, but Jason takes a step back pivoting his feet to make a full one-eighty turn. In the moment of his turn he blocks the fictitious blade turning the sword upside down and keeping with full speed he continues whirling his sword upward ripping through his opponent's body. The other three enemies attack at the same time after seeing their ally cut down in blood. Jason plunges himself backwards into the air making a full backflip like he did back at the nightclub the night he met Sabrina dodging the blades of his enemies. Coming down from the air, he angles his blade completely vertical, inserting it through the head of one of the swordsmen then turning his edge horizontal so it slices his foe entirely in half. The body splits and drops to each side. Jason swipes his blade clean of the remaining blood turning his attention toward the last two adversaries. He steps forward blocking one sword attack while bending down to dodge the other. With his sword keeping contact with the attacker on his left, he implements a side kick knocking the other flat on his back. Rotating his blade in a full circle Jason disarms his opponent and thrusts his sword through his heart. In the same motion he plants his left foot on his chest shoving them back off his sword and without looking backwards, he twirls his sword around stabbing the last enemy in the through the throat in an upward vertical thrust. Jason pulls his blade out slowly, letting gravity pull the body to the ground. Jason's illusive scenario fades from the dojo, his eyes slowly close once more, sword being sheathed and he returning to his kneeling position as he quietly whispers "De Novo."

He repeats this process over and over again several times over the course of the next few hours before Sabrina wakes up again. As she's getting out of bed, she sends a silent telepathic message to Jason while he trains letting him know of her awakening. Jason puts his blade away proceeding to make his way upstairs to the bathroom. He shuts the door behind him and, as he turns the light on his, reflection comes into view upon the mirror. Jason stops and stares at himself in the mirror for a while gazing into his dark brown eyes. He brushes the hair out of the way so he's not just peeking between the strands of his long black hair. Jason loses himself in his imagination conjuring L standing behind him. She wraps her illusionary arms around him reaching for his firm chest and her head leans on the side of his arm.

"I love you, Jason," she whispers in his ear. Jason keeps his gaze locked on himself knowing that it's just his mind running wild. "Jason, do you remember?"

"Remember?" he asks.

"Do you remember the week you stayed with me? Do you remember how we spent everyday together and held each other each night?" L asks him.

"I do remember."

"Do you remember how you said I wasn't enough for you after that week?" She takes her arms away from him and steps backwards. "During that week you somehow decided that I had no ambition for my life, and you thought I wasn't good enough for you?"

"I'm sorry L, I've told you a thousand times now."

"If I was controlling the chemicals in your body, how could you say those things to me?"

Jason's eyes widen with realization and turns around to face her but he's met with only the empty bathroom. "Jack?"

Yes, Jason? Jack answers from within his mind.

"Did you hear all that?" Jason does the same.

Yes, I did. Don't listen, it's just your broken heart playing tricks on you. Don't forget what the objective is.

"But she's right. Or I'm right?" Jason shakes his head hoping to shake his jumbled mind into place. "My imagination is right. How could I think or even say those things if she was controlling my thoughts?"

Maybe she just let her abilities damper while you were with her that week? I don't know, but she nearly had you killed by that electricity wielding guy!

"Yeah, first things first. We need to find him!" Jason says stripping the rest of his clothes off jumping into the shower washing away the sweat and pain.

Jason and Sabrina jump in Jason's black and red car and head out into the city. Sabrina, still tired from the lack of sleep, lowers her seat down and rolls over on her side closing her eyes hoping to get a little more rest. Jason glances down at her for a second and immediately experiences a flashback to when he saved her life. So much fire and death scattered around them. She succumbed to unconsciousness and lay helpless in his arms. Jason remembers how she laid sleeping next to him as he rushed her to the hospital hoping to at least save one person from that horrible tragedy. Using his adrenaline strength, Jason was able to rip her car apart to get her out, but it wasn't his strength that saved her, it was his desire to not allow anyone to suffer if he had the chance to save him. It's his whole concept behind stopping L. Jason doesn't want her to hurt anyone else the same way she hurt him. No one deserves to be manipulated and thrown away when their use runs dry.

"Sabrina, wake up, we're here." he says as he nudges her.

She pulls her seat up to an eighty-five degree angle and rubs the exhaustion from her eyes. "Here?"

"Yeah, this is where O attacked me. It was just down that alleyway there., Jason says pointing out the direction.

"Okay, let's go then," Sabrina says opening her door and stepping out.

The two walk around the corner to the empty alleyway and scan the area. They both begin looking for any kind of clues to go off. "What happened that night, Jason?"

"Well, when I first saw him he was standing right up there," Jason says pointing out the fire escape when O first called out to him. "I didn't get to see who he was. The shadows were masking his face the whole time." Jason walks over to where the fight ended. "He made a charge at me, but Jack and I fused together and grabbed him by the throat stopping him. Even though I was able to catch him, he caught me off guard I and stabbed him, and that's when I threw him against that wall," Jason says as he walks over to where he threw him. "The rain must have washed away the blood, but since there wasn't anything on the news and his body is nowhere to be found, I think it's safe to say that he got away."

"Safe wouldn't be the right word," Sabrina says in response. "You don't think he followed you or us back home, right?"

An unknown voice responds to Sabrina's question. "Not a chance! That guy was out cold for a while!" The owner of the voice stands on the same fire escape as O was the night Jason was attacked. With the sun out he's seen clearly wearing a worn out brown trench coat and a pair of ripped jeans. His brown hair is messed up, and he's clearly not had a shower in days. The bags under his eyes suggest a lack of sleep.

Jason jumps in front of Sabrina as the man suddenly jumps from atop the fire escape and uses the same technique as he to softly lower himself to the ground. "Now don't freak out!" the unknown guy says, but before he can finish his sentence, Jason already lunges at him fist cocked and adrenaline pumping. He uses his electricity abilities to zap himself into the air dodging Jason's punch and comes down on Jason with force knocking him down onto his chest. The trench coat guy steps off of Jason and walks backwards. "I'm not looking for a fight here. I jus want to talk."

Jason picks himself up off the floor kneeling down on one knee ready to attack again at a moment's notice. "Then what do you want? Are you with O?"

"As if!" The guy says in laughter. "Him and I are not even remotely on the same side!"

"Who are you then?" Sabrina asks.

"Why don't you just read my mind and find out for yourself, sweetheart?" He responded pointing at his head. Jason and Sabrina's eyes widen. "You're wondering how I know? Don't, everyone knows about you two. There's a team forming to take the both of you down, and I certainly am not on that team, I can assure you!"

"A team? What do you mean?" Jason asks.

"You two are flukes, experiments, mess ups! Don't get me wrong, I'm almost in the same boat as you two, but the one who gave you your abilities doesn't want you guys running around town like you have been, Jason."

"How do you know my name?" Jason asks standing up on his own two feet with his curiosity growing with every word this trench coat man let's through his teeth.

"I know you're Jason, and that there is Sabrina. Forgive my rudeness, my name is Rein and I'm probably the only friend you're going to have."

Jason looks back at Sabrina and then returns his focus back to Rein. "Okay, we'll bite. What's your game?"

"I'm not playing any game, Jason, I'm telling you that someone wants you dead," Rein continues while he walks closer to Jason. "I'm sure you're familiar with L, right? We all know who you are, but not all of us want to see your corpse."

"Who is 'we'?" Sabrina asks crossing her arms with skepticism.

"We as in the experiments. I don't know who He is yet, but whoever your girlfriend L is with is shacking people up in cages and giving them experimental drugs that turn them into people like O."

"O. Who is he? Why do you have the same abilities as him?" Jason demands taking a couple of steps back in mistrust.

"Because that's my power. I can copy the powers of others while I've their blood in my system. My power is the one He was trying to get for himself, but as you can see, I've escaped my cage, and now he's looking for me, too." Rein stops only six feet away from Jason. "I guess my 'game' is that I need your help."

"You need my help? What is it you think I can do for you?" Jason curiously asks.

"I need your help to stop L and Him from running these experiments on innocent people. Well, semi-innocent." Jason looks back at Sabrina for a second.

He has the same goal as we do. Sabrina says telepathically to Jason.

Or he could be lying. Jason responds then turning his attention back to Rein. "Where is O now?"

"I found him lying unconscious in this alleyway so I took his powers for my own, but before I could kill him he got away." Rein says.

"How convenient," Jason scoffs.

"If I was going to kill you, I would have done it already," Rein scoffs. "I'm on a time limit here with his powers in me, so if I was going to do something, I would have done it already!"

He's got a point, Jason, Jack says inside his head.

I don't trust him, Jason says back in the same manner. *What if this is a trap?*

Rein holds out his hand to the wall adjacent to Jason sending out zaps of electricity. With his powers he singes the wall jotting down numbers into the bricks. "That's my cell, call me when you've got some sense in your head." Rein turns his back on them, "Destroy this when you've got it down" then sends electricity through his feet, shooting upwards and disappearing atop one of the buildings.

Chapter Five

"Should we call him?" Sabrina asks Jason sitting on his bed with his number dialed into her iPhone.

"I don't know," Jason replies, staring out his window looking on at the city miles away.

"I should have delved into his mind when I had the chance, but I didn't think about it," Sabrina replies.

Well, that's ironic, isn't it? Jack says inside Jason's head. Jason just gives a chuckle in reply.

"That's not funny, Jason," Sabrina scowls.

I say we call him, Shae says inside Sabrina's head telepathically to Jason and Jack.

What if it's a trap? Jason replies inside his mind knowing that Shae can hear him.

What if it isn't? What if he truly wants to help us? Shae replies, *I mean, he didn't attack us when he had the jump on us nor did he try hiding his identity.*

"Okay," Jason says turning around. "He's the only lead we have on L. Call him, Sabrina. At least when we meet up with him, you can look inside his head to see if he's telling the truth."

"Okay," Sabrina says pressing the call button on her cell phone.

The phone gives two rings before someone on the other side answers. "Well, that didn't take too long," The voice says in the phone says.

"How did you know it was us?" Sabrina asks.

"You're the only ones I gave my number to," Rein replies.

"Ask him where he wants to meet. I don't want to stay on a public line too long," Jason directs Sabrina.

Rein, hearing Jason through the phone, immediately replies, "I'm tracking O right now actually. Meet me at The BB on Central Street downtown. That's where he is now. He's not alone either," Rein says just before he hangs up.

Sabrina lowers the phone from her head. "BB?" she asks confused.

"Alright, let's go," Jason says walking towards the door.

BB, Bourbon Bar, a place Jason knows of all too well. The bar has two levels to it's alcohol-filled environment. The whole place is filled with pool tables and two bars, one upstairs and another on the bottom floor. Jason used to hang out there after he and L went their separate ways. The weeks following his new relationship status was mostly spent within this billiards hall as he drank himself into the back seat of a taxi cab every night. Jason didn't know how to deal with L leaving him and had no one to talk to. Jason's standard for friends is so high that no one meets his requirements. His standards had to be high after being screwed over by so many people in his life. It's the same for relationships, even higher for those he picks out to be his partner.

L met those requirements though, even exceeded them. He didn't see it at the time, but when he finally saw how amazing she was, she left him. Jason theorizes that all his criticism is what actually made her leave, but of course, he won't know until he sees her again… If he sees her again.

Jason and Sabrina arrive downtown in his red and black two-toned Scion parking a few blocks away from The Bourbon Bar. "Call him." Jason says, but before Sabrina can dial the number, Rein knocks on Jason's window. Jason gets out of the car slowly, weary of Rein's actions.

"Took you long enough," Rein says.

"We don't exactly live very close to town," Jason says looking Rein up and down. "Don't you have any other clothes?" He asks noticing that Rein is wearing the same thing as yesterday.

"I don't really have a home, so it's really difficult to wash the abundance of suits in my wardrobe." Rein replies sarcastically.

Jason just rolls his eyes in reply. "C'mon, Sabrina," he says just before shutting his door. "So he's in the bar now?" Jason asks Rein.

"Yeah, I just came out of The BB," Rein replies.

"He didn't see you?"

"He doesn't know what I look like. He scurried off so quick that night he didn't bother trying to see who I was." Rein replies referring to the night Jason knocked O senseless.

The three begin walking down the street toward The BB. "So what's the plan?" Sabrina asks breaking the silence.

"Capture him of course and beat some answers out of him," Rein replies throwing punches into the air.

"That's it? That's all you've got?" Jason asks unconvinced.

"You got something better?" Rein counters.

"Yeah, I do actually. Why don't you find some way to lure him out of the bar and zap him like a stun gun knocking him unconscious, and then I'll swoop in and take him away," Jason says with pride in his voice.

"Well, here's the thing," Rein says stopping in his tracks. "I don't actually have his powers of electricity."

"What? I saw you use them yesterday," Jason says turning around to face Rein behind him.

"I only 'borrowed' his abilities for a little while. I didn't actually take him."

"Explain," Sabrina demands.

"Okay, so my abilities allow me to ingest someone else's genetic code and copy it with my own until it leaves my system," Rein explains. "When I found him, I drank some of his blood and our DNA mixed until my body completely digested his blood and broke down his DNA strand and well…" He pauses for a second, "then turned it into waste and disposed of it."

"So you're telling me that you don't have any powers to help us?" Jason growls intensely.

"That's why I said I needed your help! My power is to copy someone else's." Rein replies with a shrug of his shoulders. "You wouldn't mind if I bite you a little, would you Jason?" Rein says creating a puppy dog face in a soft begging voice.

Jason's jaw drops as his eye twitches a couple of times, "You're a sick man, Rein."

"That's how I copy someone else's powers," Rein says lowering his head in shame. "It's not my fault, that's what I was given."

Jason turns around standing still for a couple of seconds without reply. "I'll think about it," he says as he restarts his trek towards the bar.

Rein continues his walk behind him. "It'll just be a nibble. Promise!"

"You're a creep, you know that?" Jason says over his shoulder.

"He's telling the truth, Jason." Sabrina says after poking around Rein's mind.

"I don't care! He still creeps me out!"

"That's not fair…" Rein replies with a whimper.

The three arrive at the front door of The Bourbon Bar stopping for a second. "Alright, Rein, you go inside and find a way to lure him outside. He knows what I look like," Jason orders.

"I'll go with him," Sabrina says.

"No, you stay with me. I still don't trust him," Jason protests.

"I don't have any abilities Jason, I'll need her in case anything happens," Rein says in defense of Sabrina's idea.

"And if something happens!? I don't want Sabrina up there without me, and I can't go in since he knows who I am," Jason says defending his protest to the idea.

"Jason, my powers have grown. I can take care of myself." Sabrina says standing her ground.

"But…" Jason begins but is quickly cut off by Sabrina.

"Don't trust him, trust me," she persists.

Jason stands quiet, searching his mind. He battles himself for a second then looks Sabrina in the eye with intensity. "Be careful up there."

"Of course." She replies.

Jason steps back as the two enter the bar. "Shoot me a text as soon as something happens."

Sabrina simply nods her head as the door shuts behind them. She and Rein slowly take the stairs up into the dark bar. The music seems to be playing too loud and the bartender uncaringly is half dressed without any sense of decency of her appearance. A bouncer at the top stops the two of them to check their I.D.'s. Age requirements are a must for venues such as these. Sabrina gladly pulls her identification card out, but Rein is lacking one.

"You don't have an I.D.?" Sabrina asks him.

47

"I don't. I had one, but well.. I'll explain later," Rein replies. "I'll have to wait outside. Call me or Jason if anything happens," Rein takes his leave back down the stairs with a nod from Sabrina. The bouncer returns Sabrina's card, and she continues inside.

Back outside Rein steps out of the dark bar and back into the brightness of the outside sun. Much to Jason's surprise, Sabrina is not accompanying him.

"Where's Sabrina?"

"She's still in there. They didn't let me in since I don't have an I.D," Rein says back in fear of Jason's reaction.

"You left her in there alone!?" Jason frantically tries to make his way into the bar, but Rein grabs his arm advising him that O know's what he looks like, and he could compromise the ambush. "I don't care!" Jason shouts, "I can't just leave her in there by herself! It's too dangerous!"

"Jason, I told her to call us if anything happens. Plus she's in a public place, I doubt he's going to unveil his powers in there and risk his own secret." Rein's words seem to resonate with Jason calming him down.

"You're right. She'll be fine in there... I hope."

Sabrina makes her way to the bar taking up a seat. She pulls her wallet out laying down a twenty dollar bill hoping it would catch the indecently dressed bartender's attention. She waits patiently for service as she begins scanning the room. No one here in the atmosphere stands out to her at all. Everyone in the vicinity seems perfectly ordinary.

"What can I get for you, love?" the bartender asks Sabrina, resting her large breasts with seemingly overdone cleavage on the table separating the two.

Sabrina turns her attention toward the bartender, but her eyes are pulled down to stare at the bartenders' round distractions for a brief second. She closes her eyes and shakes her head back into focus bringing her gaze back up to the woman's face. "I'll take a Blue Moon if you don't mind," she replies with a flirty wink.

"You got it, babe!" The bartender says walking away but returning quickly with Sabrina's drink. "Here ya go, that'll be $4.50."

"Just take the twenty and forget about it," Sabrina quickly responds as the bartender appreciatively thanks her for her generosity. As the barkeep walks away Sabrina lifts the bottle up to her lips and sends out a telepathic message to Rein who's standing right outside. *Rein, this is Sabrina. I need to know what this guy looks like.*

Rein is jolted with astonishment as his white turns pale white. "Uh, Jason, did you hear that?"

"Hear what?" Jason asks.

"Sabrina? She just asked me what O looks like, but I must be hearing things, right?"

"She's a telepath. Just think in your head what you would say to her."

Sabrina? Rein thinks inside his head.

Yes, it's Sabrina. Give me a description of what O looks like, She replies setting her beer down on the bar without letting go.

Whoa, this is crazy! Rein replies quickly. *Do you and Jason do this a lot!?*

Later, Rein, I need to find him, I don't want to stay in here too long!

Oh, right! Okay, so.. He's tall, dark and handsome. Rein says thinking his thoughts are an adequate description.

Rein, that is NOT saying a lot. What's he wearing? Hair style? Race? Sabrina says in annoyance.

Sabrina, why do you have to involve race? You're not a racist, are you?

Sabrina places her fingers on her temples giving them a few good rubs trying not to get stressed out by him. *Rein, I can give you a migraine just by thinking about it.*

Okay, okay! O was wearing a white shirt with a black leather jacket over it. The 'cafe racer' style, not the old school 'greaser' style. I don't know why he's wearing leather in this hot weather. I think he's just trying to look cool, but those glasses of his aren't-

Sabrina cuts him off quickly not letting Rein's tangent run too long. *Okay, I see him. I'm heading in,* she says turning around with her beer in hand. As Sabrina stands up from her bar stool, the leather jacket stands up showing his blue jeans clearly and begins to walk toward the back. Sabrina tilts her head slightly, quickly pursuing him. Curiously, Sabrina delves into O's mind. *Guys, he knows who I am! He has a picture of me and recognized me!*

Jason and Rein's eyes snap to each other. "Let's go!" Jason says. Rein just gives a nod in confirmation.

Wait! He's going out through the back door! Cut him off! Sabrina tells the both of them using her telepathic powers.

Rein and Jason look around unable to stop at a nearby alleyway leading toward the back entrance. "Jason, you have the ability of super strength, right?" Rein asks looking for a solution.

"Yeah, so what?" Jason replies.

"We can use that to jump to the top of the building and get to the back faster!"

"Good idea!" He says quickly getting ready to jump but then realizes that Rein won't be able to follow. "What about you?"

"Well, give me a taste of your blood, and I'll be able to copy your DNA and gain your abilities for myself." Jason's face becomes flushed with disgust hearing Rein's proposition. "Unless you expect to carry me up there."

"Don't you even get it? It's not like I carry a knife on me."

"I've sharpened my teeth to break the skin."

"That's really creepy you know." Jason's idea of Rein's creepiness just shot up tenfold.

"I didn't ask for these abilities, ya know, I just figured out how to take advantage of it," Rein replies. Jason hesitates but eventually holds his arm our for Rein to chomp down on.

The two use the supernatural strength to leap atop the bar and back down the side. Both take their place hiding behind a couple of dumpsters waiting for O to come out the back. It doesn't take too long for him to come out as Sabrina follows quickly behind. As she and O come out, Rein and Jason pop over the green dumpsters for the ambush.

"That's far enough, O! We've got you outnumbered so just surrender!" Jason shouts out as his feet meet the ground.

"What he said!" Rein adds.

"So, you're still alive, are you, Rein? The director figured you wouldn't last too long on your own, but here you are!" O says in a cocky voice. "And you made friends! How cute!"

"Don't patronize me!" Rein shouts. "But yes, and now me and my 'friends' are going to kick your ass!"

"Don't be so arrogant, Rein!" O replies. "What makes you think that I don't have friends of my own?" He says as two others bust through the door behind Sabrina. The both of them grab Sabrina by her arms restraining her from escaping. "Now what will you two do huh?"

"Sabrina!" Jason calls out with concern.

"Just give up, these two can kill her in a second." O turns around walking toward his two friends and Sabrina. He places his hand on her face, looking Jason in the eye "How horrible would it be if I just sent a thousand volts through her body right now frying her internal organs, killing her from the inside out?"

Jason steps forward but O shocks Sabrina's face in determent. "Don't you dare take another step, or she dies!" Hearing this, Sabrina uses her telekinesis powers to create a forceful push sending the three thugs, including O, flying away from her in separate directions. The three slam into nearby walls with great pain.

"How horrible would it be if I just killed each of you without even lifting a finger?" Sabrina says with a hint of scoff in her voice. She slowly makes her way over to Jason and Rein, taking her place between them.

"Sabrina, I didn't know you had that kind of power!" Jason says trying to keep his jaw from dropping to the floor.

"You're not the only one that trains in their spare time you know."

O and the others pick themselves up off the floor. "That's pretty impressive, I didn't think such a small girl would have such a painful bite!" He says as the three regroup with each other. "This is going to be fun!"

O sparks electricity through his fingers gearing up for the fight that's about to commence. "My two friends come equipped appropriately just as I have," O says placing his hands down by his sides. "Sid here," he says motioning to the plain black and blue jeans wearing thug to his right, "is able to control and manipulate fire by tweaking his own body's temperature." Then motioning to the guy on his right, who's dressed in what appears to be the same kind of jeans but also appareled in a black hoodie, explains his abilities. "He can control the H2O in the air making water of any kind his tool of destruction." Turning his attention back to Jason and his own friends, he adds "You don't want to do this. Trust me."

Rein retaliates in anger without thinking. "Like we would trust you! You're the enemy!"

"Rein, he was being sarcastic," Jason says shaking his head in disappointment.

"I knew that!" Rein replies.

"You're coming with us, one way or another!" Sabrina says ignoring the bickering between Jason and Rein.

"We'll see, baby doll!" O says as the hoodie wearing thug concentrates on bringing the water in the air together creating a sphere of water. O sends a jolt of electricity into the sphere making it dangerously electrified as Sid adds an atmospheric heat around the same ball of water making a combined elemental attack. "Let's see how well you handle this!" O shouts out as the ball of elements is shot out with high velocity!

Chapter Six

Rein and Jason leap out in front of Sabrina throwing their arms out hoping to protect her as much as they can with their enhanced strength. Both close their eyes waiting for the devastating impact which never occurs. Slowly their eyes peel back the darkness revealing the combined elemental ball suspended in front of them. Jason looks at Rein as he does the same in confusion. The two turn their attention past the ball toward O and his thugs as the three stand astonished.

Jason turns his head around lowering his arms to see Sabrina hovering above them, arms out, and palms out. "Sabrina?"

"I'm not as weak as you think, Jason," She says giving a confident wink. She brings her palms together as though holding a ball between her hands then bringing the two halves together causing the ball elements to explode in a contained barrier she's created around it.

Rein turns around after witnessing the ball explode into nothing. "That was awesome, Sabrina!" He says throwing his arms up into the air in excitement. "Now let's kick their ass, Jason!"

"Right!" Jason replies as the two rush toward O and his men. *Jack, don't worry about giving me your strength! This is what I've been training for!*

Jason throws a right hook toward O but swings right over his head as O ducks under. Jason, using his gained momentum, follows up swinging his left leg around and collides it with O's ribs. Sid catches O from toppling over and immediately ignites his fist in flames thrusting it forward at Jason who seamlessly side steps to avoid them. Behind him Rein is throwing punch after punch at the hooded guy but each attack is blocked by quickly conjured walls of water forming around him.

"That's not fair!" Rein yells out in frustration. "You can't just keep making water over and over!"

"Keep punching all you want! Each punch you throw only douses you in more and more water!" The hood says laughing with his arms crossed. Rein pauses for a brief second, cocking his arm at his side and focusing on his new found strength from Jason. After a brief moment, Rein releases his fist punching through a thick water wall separating the hood and Rein and quickly connecting with the hood's face, knocking him back up against the brick wall behind him. Without hesitation he springs forward grabbing the guy by the neck and tossing him aside propelling his body at least thirty feet down the alleyway.

Jason grabs onto O's shoulder using him as support so he can take three steps on the wall and over O's body. As Jason is coming down, his right foot connects with Sid's shoulder sending him straight to the ground. Rein turns around rushing over to the three as Sid hits the flow. Without a second thought, Jason grabs hold of O's arms restraining him. Rein gears up to impact O's abs with his fists, but before he can make contact, O electrifies his body stunning Jason and sending Rein flying backward in the hood's direction.

"Jason!" Sabrina yells out. Jason shakes his head raising his hand toward Sabrina in a "I'm okay" motion, but before Jason can collect himself, O turns to the side kicking Jason in the chest then following up with a roundhouse dropping Jason to the ground. By this time Sid has picked himself up off the ground, turning his attention toward the fallen Jason. Sid extends his arm out toward Jason and, suddenly flames spontaneously combust and rage toward Jason. Jason rolls out of the way popping himself back to his feet. Without missing a single beat he dances his way backwards dodging each fiery ball shot at him. O starts sending out shocks as Sid's flames still ignite around Jason. Unable to keep up with each attack, Jason stumbles backwards into a sitting position as a bolt of electricity and ball of flames are plummeting toward him.

Rein, slowly regaining his consciousness, makes his way to his feet, "Shocking!" Without a single reply from anyone, Rein chuckles to himself at his own bad joke. He looks over at Jason tilting his head curiously for a second.

"You have bad jokes!" The hooded guy says behind him, but before turning around, he's kicked in the back without budging. "What the hell!?"

"Wow, that's nice!" Rein says turning around toward his enemy. "That guy over there, he has enhanced strength, and I can copy that power, but I didn't know that pain wasn't an issue with his ability." After explaining this, Rein throws another punch, but without knowing the strength he possesses, his fist is sent completely through the hood's chest breaking his ribs and ripping through organs in the way. "Holy crap! I just…" Rein slowly pulls his arm out of his foe's chest as the life leaves the body.

Jason throws his arms up as if to block the attacks by Sid and O. Without feeling a thing, Jason slowly opens his eyes to the flames dissipating and the bolt of electricity not even existent. "What the heck?" Jason picks himself up off the ground as the two send out more elemental attacks, but each one is stopped by an invisible wall in front of Jason. "What is this?" Jason asks out loud noticing none of the attacks can reach him.

"Don't worry Jason, I've got this!" Sabrina yells out.

"Thanks, Sabrina!" Jason says then springs forward quickly toward the two. O shoots himself upwards into the sky using the electricity as propulsion, landing safely on a nearby fire escape ladder. Jason comes face to face with Sid and starts throwing punch after punch breaking through each one of Sid's blocks. Jason collides with Sid and rams his fist into Sid's stomach knocking the wind out of him. In retaliation, Sid ignites his fists firing up to counter but Jason lowers his body to the ground and using his coffee grinder technique, kicking Sid's legs out from underneath him. Sid falls down on his shoulder, letting out a cracking sound causing him to let out a painful screech.

Jason gets back up to his feet looking onward to where Rein is standing. Jason calls out to him, but Rein doesn't respond. Jason looks closer noticing, a body lying on the floor without movement, and Rein staring at his own upheld hand. O, noticing the stillness of Rein, turns his attention to him shooting bolts of electricity. "Rein!" Jason calls out darting forward, "Move!" Sabrina, knowing Jason won't get there in time, levitates one of the nearby dumpsters toward Rein, but with the quickness of the bolts she's not fast enough either. Two bolts hit Rein in back knocking him on top of the lifeless body in front of him.

Jason, seeing Rein fall to the floor before Sabrina's dumpster can block the other attacks, fills with rage inside. Jason leaps over the dumpster, grabbing Rein, and lifting him off the hood's body. "Rein! Talk to me, Rein!" Jason says frantically, but receives no response. Sid picks himself up off the floor taking hold of his shoulder. He tries removing his hand, but the pain is too much making him keep his hand holding his shoulder.

Unable to use his hands, Sid can't use his fire element. "Damn it, I can't do anything," he says looking onward at Jason and Rein behind the dumpster.

"Sid, what're you doing!? Attack!" O shouts from up high.

"I can't! My shoulder is broken, I think," Sid shouts back.

"I don't care! L told you to be useful to me, and I'm telling you to kill them!"

Listen to whatever O tells you, Sid, L's voice resonates inside Sid's head remembering what she told him. *Do whatever he asks of you. For me.* Sid turns his attention back to the two behind the dumpster and starts running toward them. With each step Sid takes, his body becomes more and more covered in flames. Soon, before reaching them, his whole body is ignited in flames burning off his clothes, singing his skin and burning away his hair.

"Jason!" Sabrina calls out grabbing his attention. "Behind you!" Jason turns his attention toward the flaming Sid racing toward them. "Use your powers!" Sabrina shouts stretching her hand out toward him.

"But the repercussion!?" Jason shouts back as Sid leaps into the air over the dumpster Jason is kneeling down behind.

"Just do it, Jason! Trust me!" Hearing Sabrina's words he puts all his faith in her. The adrenaline shoots throughout his entire body bulking up each of his muscles. With his increased strength he leaps toward Sid in the air grabbing him by the neck almost crushing the cervical curvature of his vertebrae. As the adrenaline rushes through Jason's body, his senses heighten. With his increased senses, he hears a small crack from Sid's body and loosens his grip around his neck. The adrenaline also causes his brain to think at an incredible speed causing him to consider his ability to kill him Sid.

While he's in the air, Jason launches Sid's flaming body at O atop the fire escape at a high velocity. O, concluding that his comrade won't survive his body's burns, protects himself by electrifying Sid's body diverting its projectile course. The shock given by O fries Sid's body even more as his body hits a nearby wall letting out loud cracks from all over his body. Jason lands safely back on the ground as Sid's body comes crashing down with even more bone breaking sounds.

The adrenaline in Jason's body begins to recess as he notices Sabrina's body fall out of the air. With the last of his body's enhanced strength, he darts over to her, catching her before hitting the ground. With the adrenaline completely absent from Jason's body, he collapses from fatigue causing both he and Sabrina to fall to the ground.

"Looks like I won!" O says feeling proud of himself for beating Jason and his companions. "Would you kindly just sit still as I kill you both."

"That's not going to happen," A voice says from behind O. He turns around as quick as he can with fear overtaking his body, but the fear turns to astonishment as he finds Rein standing behind him. O electrifies his hands but before he can execute an attack, Rein kicks him off the fire escape sending him flying toward the ground. That one kick knocks O unconscious leaving him unable to use his powers to catch himself.

Jason looks up and, over Sabrina's body, sees O fall to the ground. "Don't let him die!" Rein hearing his words jumps over the ledge of the roof and shoots himself down to the ground breaking the concrete beneath him as he lands underneath O catching him. Seeing O in Rein's arms relieves Jason as he passes out from the fatigue caused by his body's adrenaline.

"Jason! Tell them about the time we pretended we were on an Indiana Jones ride!" L shouts from a couch with two others. L is accompanied by Valentine and James.

"Okay, okay, you two are gonna love this!" Jason says walking into the living room from the kitchen with a couple of beers for Valentine and James. He hands off the beers to them then takes a few steps back. "So there we were, driving down Coors on our way to the movie theatre. Well, we had like half an hour to kill so I get this great idea!"

"Yeah, from me!" L interrupts excitingly.

"So it was an inspired idea," Jason says scratching the back of his head. "She had told me she never been to DisneyLand. 'So you've never been on the Indiana Jones ride?' I ask her and, of course, she said no." Jason brings both his hands to his side, aligned with his shoulders and palms up. "Of course she hasn't been on the ride if she's never been to DisneyLand."

"Well, duh, Jason!" Valentine replies sarcastically.

"Anyway! With half an hour on our hands, I pull off the road and head down to an empty dirt lot. I park the car and shut the lights off! I grab my phone out and YouTube the famous Indiana Jones theme song!" Jason takes a drink of his nearby Blue Moon placing it back down clearing his throat at the same time. "L looks at me confused as I press play on my phone, and I just tell her 'get ready for an adventure,' and the song slowly creeps into the speakers!" Jason says excitingly placing both hands out in front of him pretending he's holding his car's steering wheel. "I rev my engine a few times as the music gets louder and louder and finally when the music kicks in, I turn the lights on and hit the gas! I'm driving left and right in the dirt, pulling the hand brake to power slide!"

"The whole time he's narrating the thing with jewel thieves after us, cliffs we're driving over, and scary caves we're driving through." L adds, almost matching Jason's excitement.

"And then when the music is almost about to end, I stop the car abruptly with dust kicked up all around us and L laughing from the fun! She looks over at me and I to her with these big cheesers on our faces!" Jason looks over to L sitting on the couch, mixed drink in hand, and her big brown eyes looking at him with love. "Then I turn my face to fear! She tries matching mine. I look to the front of the car and give out a small yell, 'Oh, no! A huge boulder is coming our way!' She looks forward with me as I toss the gear in reverse speeding backwards." Jason is looking forward and backward trying his hardest to animate his story. "You know, the infamous boulder that he runs from in that one movie!?"

"Yeah! Yeah!" James says in response.

"The music dies, and I stop the car again with dust everywhere. I look over at L and tell her that I would take her on the real thing someday, but she just looks back at me as her laughing begins to slow down and says, 'Jason, you're the best,' and she gives me a kiss."

"What's worse is he had just washed his car that day too!" L adds on at the end of Jason's story, "But he didn't even care that his car was dirty again." L says smiling at Jason.

"That sounds like it would be hella fun!" Valentine says.

Jason turns his head giving it a couple of scratches in embarrassment. As he opens his eyes, he notices a strange picture on the wall of his apartment. "Huh?" Jason drops his hand to his side examining the picture. "Sabrina?" He says under his breath. Jason looks over at L on the couch and back at the picture. It's him and Sabrina in the picture. They're both wearing white lab coats working with chemicals and computers. In the picture Sabrina is standing behind Jason as he's holding out his hand behind him and a paper in the other. Jason looks back at L on his couch. She's laughing and smiling with James and Valentine as his apartment becomes brighter and brighter. Soon his whole vision is engulfed in a bright white light. He brings his hands up rubbing the brightness from his eyes.

"I told you not to look into the microscope until you calibrated the light." Sabrina says walking over to Jason in her white lab coat.

"I forgot. Do you have the sample?" Jason responds holding his hand out behind him as he picks up a lab report reading its inscriptions.

"Yeah, here's the blood sample from L," Sabrina says handing Jason a small vial.

Jason places the report down grabbing the vile from her. He drips a couple drops under the lens, analyzing it. "How is she doing anyway?"

Sabrina cringes for a second. "Does it matter?"

Jason lifts his eyes from the lens and turns around slowly. "Sabrina," He says. Sabrina just turns her head and gives a "humph" in reply. He grabs her by the hand pulling her in. "You know I love you and only you, but we need to make sure she's okay. We need her so we can find a cure."

"She's fine," Sabrina says as she keeps her head turned away.

"Okay, now let's get back to work." Jason says letting go of her hand as he turns back around. "Can you cross examine the blood from O with mine to find similarities?"

"Yeah," She replies walking over to her desk. There's silence between the two of them, the air thickens with tension.

Jason senses this getting up from his chair. He walks over to Sabrina placing his arms around her from behind placing his chin on her shoulder. In a low whisper he asks, "Do you love me?"

"Of course, I do," Sabrina says raising her hands off the table placing them on Jason's arms around her. He gives her a small kiss on the cheek then turning her around.

"We stopped L's powers, you don't have to worry about her messing with my chemicals again," Jason grabs her hands. "I love you, Sabrina, and only you." Jason leans up giving her a kiss, but as he pulls away, she grabs the back of his head not wanting him to stop.

Jason returns and begins to kiss her more intently. Their body temperatures rise as the pheromones between them follow suit. Jason rises over her grabbing her by her thighs lifting her onto the table. While kissing her he kicks the chair away crawling on top of her tearing off his lab coat. Their kissing becomes more intense as he places her hands on his back dragging her nails down. Slowly Jason reaches for the back of her head intertwining his hands with her hair, and his other hand slides under her lower back lifting her up as he leans back into a sitting position placing her on top of him.

Sabrina slides off his shirt revealing his bare body. Jagged abs, small firm chest, slender curvatures. She leans back to get a better look placing both her palms on his chest biting her lip in desire. She runs her hands up and down his chest then sliding them across his side and to his back pulling him in closer. He bites down on her neck sliding her lab coat off. Jason tosses her coat next to his own and then rips off her black and white plaid shirt. Jason pulls her in closer as she bites down on his neck, nails riding down his back and her legs wrapping around him. Jason's eyes open in excitement, but what he sees brings his excitement to a stop.

Hanging on the wall behind her is a picture of himself in his apartment. In the picture it shows James, Valentine and L sitting on his couch, and he's standing up in front of them with his arms out. They all seem to be having a great time and laughing. "What the hell?" Jason says under his breath. "Why is that here?"

"Why is what here?" Sabrina's breath heavy and fatigued with desire. The lab they're in begins to brighten immersing Jason's vision in nothing but a white light once again. Jason's vision recovers, and he's back in his apartment with the three in the picture.

Back in the apartment Jason looks up at L whose smiling back at him. He gives a smile back to her but turns his head to look at the picture on the wall which displays himself and Sabrina kissing on a lab table. Again, his vision is engulfed in white as the room fades away, although he doesn't return to the lab with Sabrina. Instead his white vision seems to be swallowed up by darkness in a swirling fashion until it's completely gone. There's nothing but darkness around him as he hears a faint voice in the distance, "Jason."

"Who's there?" he asks.

"Jason," the voice says louder. "Jason," the voice says once more even louder.

Jason brings his hands up rubbing his eyes as he blinks the underside of a bridge into existence. Jason opens his eyes, and sees Sabrina over him.

"You're finally awake!" Sabrina says.

"Sabrina?" Jason replies.

"Yeah, it's me, and we're okay."

Jason slowly raises his hand placing his palm on the side of her cheek slowly sliding it up to her head intertwining his fingers with her hair.

Sabrina becomes confused with her face openly expressing it. She peers down at him with longing. "Jason?"

Chapter Seven

Violet and pink coat the sky as the sun slowly begins to set. The breeze of the wind kicks up leaves spiraling in every direction. Jason removes his hand from Sabrina's hair bringing it to the front of his head. Pounding and aching within, he closes his eyes trying to concentrate.

"Are you okay?" Sabrina asks.

"I've got a splitting headache," Jason lifts himself up from his back scooting back to lean his back on a wall underneath the bridge they're under. "Must be from the adrenaline."

Jason looks around noticing the makeshift home around him. Sheets spread over openings of cardboard walls, crates filled with stolen canned foods, torn clothes hanging from atop a wire, and a fire blazing in control centered within the makeshift home. "Where are we, Sabrina?"

"Rein brought us here," Sabrina looks over at Rein sitting by the fire. "I don't exactly know where we are. I was unconscious like you when we arrived."

"What happened? Where's O?"

"Rein has him tied up and unconscious in the back." She turns back to Jason. "I'm not entirely sure what happened though. Rein hasn't said a word since I woke up."

"I'll go talk to him." Jason gets up dusting himself off as he walks over to Rein. He's just sitting there, staring into the fire. No expressions on his face, barely moving at all, not even turning to Jason as he approaches. Jason sits down next to Rein staring into the fire with him without saying a word.

Jason had spent time studying the energy within the human body. That feeling two people get on a first date, or when people fight and somehow find a way to calm down without resolve, or even when two lovers share each other in the dark are all examples of energy communication. No words exchanged, only the bodies speaking to each other.

Jason clears his mind allowing his energy to flow freely. The fire cracks and sparks, the wind ruffles the sheets over the cardboard walls and the sun inches further and further out of sight. Rein scratches the back of his head then cracking his knuckles. Jason gives him a short look then back at the fire.

"They're dead," Rein says in a low, barely audible voice.

"Yeah, They are," Jason replies in the same manner.

"I didn't mean to kill him. I didn't know how strong I was." Rein lifts up his hand in front of him staring into his palm. "My fist went through his body."

"It's not your fault." Jason places his hand on Rein's shoulder. "They were trying to kill us, too."

"I knew him. That guy in the hood. His name was Aaron," Rein hangs his head dropping his hand to his side.

Jason pulls his hand off of Rein's shoulder. "How did you know him?"

"We were prisoners. Kept in cages, kept in the dark. I didn't realize it until I killed him, but he was there with me."

"With you where?"

"I don't know. Even now I can't remember where that place is, but there were quite a few of us all chained up." Rein picks his head up gazing at Jason. "We were both prisoners and I killed him. We suffered the same, and he died at my hand." A tear rolls down Rein's face. He quickly wipes it away turning his head in the opposite direction.

"I need you to tell me about this place, Rein." Jason says sounding concerned. "What was it?"

"About a year ago I was kidnapped. Picked up off the side of the road. I was hitch hiking and got into the wrong car evidently," Rein looks around. "I've been here for a couple of weeks now since I escaped."

"Hmmm," Jason leans back on both his hands listening intently.

"The guy that picked me up pulled over for gas, but right after he parked, he knocked me out and I woke up in chains."

Rein had woken within the dark, legs and arms bound in metal chains. His vision quickly adapted to the dark and realized he was in a cage meant for a large dog. He freaked and started to shout calling for help. Someone else was in the room with him though. Told him to shut up and calm down or things would get worse for him.

"Who's there!?" Rein calls out frantically.

"My names' Aaron. You need to stop panicking and settle in. You'll be here a while." Just as Aaron said, Rein spent a year of his life in and out of his cage. Frequently taken into a lab strapped to a bed, with needles, chemicals and gases being pumped into his body. As the days passed, Rein noticed changes in himself. Some nights he would be in extreme pain from his body's insides changing, and other nights he could feel a tingling in his body adaptations.

After a while, he and Aaron were separated. After their separation, Rein was occasionally placed in a room with nothing but a one way mirror. Inside, Rein and one other would be pitted against each other. He and his first opponent were hesitant to fight at first, but a voice over an intercom said that if they didn't fight, they would both be executed. So they fought. Beat each other to a pulp. Rein lost his first fight. Knocked out in the room, he was taken unconsciously back to his cage and then the next day was experimented on again. It would happen over and over again. He would be forced to fight someone, whether he won or lost, he was taken and experimented on, thrown back in his cage and forced to fight again and again with experiments after every fight.

After some time of this repetitive routine, Rein was given a small tablet about an hour before the fight. He was placed in the arena again and fought his opponent as usual. This fight was different though, after a couple of minutes in, his opponent disappeared. Nowhere to be seen. Even though his enemy couldn't be seen, Rein was still attacked. Punched and kicked left and right from thin air. Eventually he was knocked out again. This time there was no experiment afterwards. Only placed in his cage and thrown back into the arena again a few days later. Every fight he had after that was entirely different. Each opponent he fought had some kind of supernatural abilities. Some shot fire from their hands, others were as quick as a hare, or even able to instantaneously disappear and reappear in a different place in the room.

Rein couldn't believe what he was seeing. Every enemy he fought had some kind of supernatural ability that he just couldn't compete with. From here on out, he lost every match that came his way. The pills they were giving him seemed to have no effect on his body which made him curious as to what they were. Placebos maybe? It wasn't until his last fight where he figured out what he could do.

During his last fight, he went up against an opponent who could manipulate the temperature in the air to subzero degrees. His enemy put up quite the fight and Rein thought for sure he was going to lose once again. The ice wielder began by just toying around with him, freezing his arms, his legs, eventually freezing him against the arena wall. Rein thought for sure his demise was imminent until the enemies frosted hand gripped his throat giving him the opportunity to chomp down on his arm. Rein's teeth sunk in so deep blood began dripping from the side of his mouth. As the blood ran into Rein's mouth and down the back of his throat, there was a chilling sensation following closely behind. The temperature in his body dropped rapidly, his breath like ice, the dripping blood begin to freeze. Rein, confused by the sudden phenomenon, just bit harder out of fear causing his enemy's whole body to freeze over in seconds. Rein unclenched his jaw and the opponent fell over, his body shattering like glass. Before Rein could process what happened, the lights went out, bag thrown over his head and drug out of the arena by what felt like five people.

Back in his cell, Rein thought about his fight with the ice guy. Everyone he fought had some sort of special abilities, those pills given to him before each fight, himself not having powers like the others. "When I bit into that guy, and his blood went in my mouth, I could do what he did." He whispered to himself in his cage. "I need to try again tomorrow."

Just as usual, the white coats gave him another pill just before his next fight. His new opponent could manipulate the growth rate of her bones. As soon as the lights came on Rein found himself being charged by a young girl, around the same age as him, with three inch long spikes coming out of her hands and before he has time to react, she stabbed him in the shoulder. Immediately seeing his opportunity, Rein took hold of her arm and chomped down as hard as he could, drawing blood into his mouth gulping it down. As the blood entered his system, Rein could feel his body's genetic makeup transform. Bones from every which way began to bust out of his body. He let go of her and jumped backwards wailing in pain. "I can't stop it!" Rein shouted. His spinal cord grew out of his back, ribs increasing in size, and his fingers' bones sprouting like weeds.

Rein wails and wails in excruciating pain unable to handle his skin being broken every which way. His opponent rushes to his side rapping her arm around the back of his shoulders. "Just breathe!" she says panicking. "Stay calm! Focus on my voice!" Rein's head is shaking back and forth, his ears unable to hear her words. The girl starts to rub his head, whisper softly in his ear, "It's going to be okay, you're safe now!" The shaking in Rein's body slowly calms, his heartbeat slows, and she's just holding him. The bones in his body stop growing. The pain is still there, but the bones have ceased.

Rein looks up into her big brown eyes, innocent and caring. "Thank you." The girl just smiles back at him. "What's your name?" Rein asks, hands and knees on the floor and her arm around him.

"Its Valentine," she says just before the lights go out and bags over each of their heads.

"Valentine?" Jason asks in astonishment. "Blonde hair and brown eyes?" He continues. *It can't be the same Valentine, can it?*

"Yeah, it was through her that I realized what kind of abilities I had. Being able to copy someone else's for a brief amount of time comes in handy." He makes his mouth into a smile revealing his two razor sharp canine teeth at the top of his mouth. "I used her powers to grow out my two canine teeth so I could easily get anyone's blood and copy their powers." Rein looks to his fire. "That's how I escaped."

After his fight with Valentine, Rein was operated on removing the excess bones and sealing up the wounds they created in his body. He was placed back in his cage shortly thereafter where he had awoken. "Valentine," he whispers to himself. "She's just a prisoner like me, like the rest of us here. Being made to fight and experimented on." He shifts to lay on his side staring into the endless darkness. "I have got to get out of here." His body curls up into an almost fetal position, "Valentine too." The darkness expands around him shrouding his entire sight as he drifted off to sleep.

Rein continued to fight, continued to copy the abilities of others, losing some while winning most of his fights. After a while of this tedious routine, he started making viles out of the supplies he was given when he was given food everyday. During his fights he would store some of the enemies' blood and keep it for later use. Storing ammo for later, each bullet carrying a different ability to use in his arsenal. Rein becomes more used to using other's powers as he learned to control them while not letting them take him out.

"But didn't the stored blood you collected go bad or something?" Jason asks sitting next to Rein by the fire.

"Yeah, and I learned that the hard way." Rein was planning on escaping one night, drinking the blood of an opponent who could turn himself invisible, but his powers were lacking. He tried another vile of blood and another and another, but still nothing. *The blood must have gone bad,* he thought to himself. *Damn, without it being cold, it doesn't last very long, I guess,* Rein gathered from homicide shows he used to watch. Rein bided his time until his next fight which he was sure was going to be in a couple of days since the fights only occurred about twice a week, or at least that's what he thought, as a lack of a calendar would mesh his days into countless numbers.

Instead of another fight, he was actually taken to an operating room, bag over his head, two guys, one on each arm, carrying him to a cold, sterile room full of light and white coats. "This is the copy-cat, sir," one white coat said.

"Take the bag off his head, I want to see his face," a voice over the intercom ordered and just like that, the bag was removed placing his eyes to stare into his own reflection. Another one way mirror. Someone watching him as he watched himself try to pierce the veil of its reflection. Arms and legs bound, mouth gagged, Rein was unable to move or speak. The man behind the mirror ordered for my blood to be drawn and examined. "I want to know what it is about this one that allows him to copy the other experiments."

They took his blood, filling vile after vile until Rein eventually passed out. When he woke up, the bag was once again over his head, and he was strapped to a table. He woke up very slowly without movement or noise. "Did you hear, the boss is dispatching a team to take out Rogue One," the man above Rein said, as he pushed Rein along on a bed with straps.

"So he finally found him, huh? Rogue One is his pet's ex-boyfriend right?" Another asked in reply.

"Yeah, I guess that girl L gave him some of the experimental drug before she broke up with him. 'Least that's what I heard anyway."

"Damn, the boss must've been pretty pissed, huh?"

"The boss said he was going to send Osiris and two others after Rogue One."

"Shit! Osiris!? That electric guy? Oh, man, Rogue One is gonna be dead without ever knowing what hit him!"

The conversation between the two slowly diverted into sports and barbecues, plans which were being made for later. *Rogue One? If the "boss" is worried about this guy, I've got to find him,* Rein thought to himself as the two guards conversation went on.

"Is he still passed out?" A guard asked as he poked the side of Rein. He didn't move a muscle, just stay laying there.

"I think so."

"Good, makes our job easier. No squirming or nothin', just toss em' in the cage."

The straps were being undone, first the legs and up to the arms, then finally the strap over Rein's chest came off. The guards lifted him up into a sitting position and slowly put their shoulder under each arm of Rein. Immediately Rein pulled both of them in bashing their heads against each other. He clocked one straight in the nose and brought his arm backward colliding his elbow into the other guard's face. Rein jumped off the table, pulling the bag off his head, and pushed the table on top of one of the guards. Without hesitation, he slammed the heel of his foot into the jaw of the other guard breaking his jaw. Meanwhile the other pushed the table off springing up to his feet hitting Rein in the back with a black nightstick. Rein, being used to pain due to all his fighting, turned around as though nothing had happened. He grabbed the guard's shoulders tight jumping on top of him as the guard fell to his back and bit into his jugular with his newly sharpened teeth thanks to Valentine. His blood flowed like a river causing his life to spill out and down Rein's throat.

Rein, covered in blood, got up to his feet and stood in front of his cage. "This will be the last time I see these bars," he said quietly and just walked away. He walked down a dark corridor searching for an exit and trying to be as silent as physically possible. He placed his ear against each door he came across, the echoing words behind a door he ignored, but any with silence within he entered.

He entered one room of silence, but found nothing but an operating table and surgical equipment. Another was filled with stethoscopes, needles, and other such experimental objects. Rein then proceeded to enter a room that was filled with other prisoners, each locked up like he was. He turned to leave but stopped just before turning the knob of the door to this room. *What if they have abilities?* Rein thought to himself.

He turned and walked slowly to a cage laced with gold looking wire around the entire cage. They were electrified, but not in the shocking way if someone were to touch them. Reaching into the sleeping prisoners cage he grabbed his arm slowly pulling it between the bars. As he held the forearm of the prisoner in both his hands Rein sunk his sharpened canines in shaking his head back and forth digging them deeper drinking the blood. The prisoner woke up kicking and screaming pulling his arm away from Rein's bloody hands. As the caged man cried for help, he would disappear and reappear within his cage. A siren went off and the entire room was lit up by red rotating lights contained in bulbs sticking out of the walls. "Shit!" Rein darted off quickly out the doors and down the corridor which was no longer dark but drenched in red and screeching sirens. Rein was panicking taking every possible turn becoming more lost in this labyrinth of a building.

Within minutes of his running around he started to run into guards at every turn. Eventually he was surrounded by them, at least eight guards had him cornered all dressed in black with caps on which read "Security" on the forefront. One of them held a gun at Rein and shot him with some kind of dart. He immediately pulled the dart out as the security guard lowered his gun. Rein's legs became weak while his vision blurred. He fell to his knees holding the shoulder where he was shot. "Damn it," Rein said as he fell to the ground closing his eyes. His eyes opened again seeing the guards walking toward him, one holding handcuffs and the others ready with nightsticks. He blinked a few times, each time the guards closer and closer. The last time he blinked, he caught the sight of a cement wall in front of him. *What?* He thought to himself blinking a few more times to see if it was actually a wall. Each time his eyes opened all he saw was cement in front of him. He rolled onto his side making the last thing he saw before passing out was a bridge over him and a night sky filled with stars.

"I guess that person I bit into had the ability to teleport." Rein said turning his head away from the fire bringing his eyes to meet Jason's. "This is where I found myself when I woke up and spent about a month under this bridge."

"So you have no idea where this institute is?" Sabrina asked standing behind Jason.

"I don't, but I do know that Osiris, or O as you know him as, was being prepped to come after you." Rein explained. "Eventually I found him and the two others and kept my eyes on them knowing it would lead me to you. To Rogue One."

"And L? Did you see her at all in that place?" Jason asked.

Rein turned his head back toward the fire, then looking up to the stars. "No, but as they called her the boss's pet, I'm guessing she's his squeeze or something." Jason lowered his head in sadness. Sabrina placed her arms on his shoulders, but sad that she could see how hurt Jason was over L.

"Let's get as much information as we can out of Osiris," Jason says without looking up.

Chapter Eight

The Sinclair mansion is quiet. The sun, barely rising, heating the cool of the morning soothes Sabrina as she opens the creaking front door. She enters slowly, checking the corners for any signs of life, "Christós?" she keeps looking around making sure he's still asleep in his bed, "Christós?" After a few seconds of recon she gives the go ahead for the boys to enter. Jason and Rein enter behind her each having an arm of Osiris around their necks. Osiris' feet are bound, his mouth gagged, still knocked out from the previous night at Rein's make-shift home. Sabrina shuts the wooden door behind them when an old rotary phone goes off with a loud, eardrum busting ring. Sabrina is given a jump scare really quick but rapidly calms herself down. "Why do we still have this phone?" She mumbles to herself as she answers. "Hello?"

"Sabrina, it's Chris, I won't be home until later this evening. Something at work came up. I'll see you later, little sister." Before Sabrina can give a reply the line goes dead, and she's left with nothing but a dial tone. Sabrina slowly lowers the phone back down. She turns to the guys slowly. "That was my brother. He won't be home until later this evening so we're clear for a while."

"Perfect," Jason says. "At least we won't have to worry about explaining anything for right now."

"Is there somewhere we can... question O?" Rein asks suspiciously.

"Yeah, we actually have a cellar behind the mansion."

"That'll be perfect!" He replies taking Osiris to the back of the mansion with the help of Jason. Rein's surprise can't be hidden when the backyard falls upon his eyes. Three acres of land lay before him; an unimaginable field of space to a young lad who had spent his time scraping by under a bridge. A swimming pool rests under a waterfall made of granite equipped with a diving board and poolside accessories. Across is a stable housing a few horses and a sheep dog pacing back and forth from end to end. The rest is covered in bright green grass and a shed toward the back.

"There's a basement through that door over there," Sabrina motions to the shed across the way, and the boys carry O onward. "We hardly go down there anymore, except when we need something out of storage… Which we never do."

"How can your family afford all this?" Rein asks as they pace across the large yard.

"Our family is… was ambitious," Sabrina replies.

"Was?" Jason questions.

"My parents passed away sometime ago as I've said, but ever since I don't really know what I want to do with myself as far as expanding my parent's companies." Sabrina looks away across her open field. "The companies pretty much run themselves, and I'm supposed to take over but that means me doing a whole lot of nothing since there's already managers in place, and all I have to do is watch the money deposit into our family account every month."

"And your brother?" Rein goes on.

"He's doing his own thing. He always says he's working, but he never tells me what he does." Sabrina's melancholy on the issue is easily heard. "To be honest, I don't really care what he does with his time. He drowns himself in his 'work' so much that he never makes any time for me." Sabrina clears a strand of hair from her face placing the black thread comfortably behind her ear. "I used to be here by myself ever since my parents died, but having Jason here has been really nice," She adds cracking a smile.

Yeah, but like her brother, I'm so caught up in my training that it's like I'm not even here either, Jason thinks to himself.

Rein and Jason strap O to a chair in the basement making sure he's completely secured. "Alright, wake him up. Sabrina, I'll need you to suppress his powers," Jason orders.

"Right," She says with a nod. She holds up her hands in Osiris' direction closing her eyes. Immediately her eyes shoot open realizing he's not like them. "Jason, he doesn't have a second persona inside!"

"What do you mean?"

"I mean it's just him in there."

"But if that's the case how does he have his electrical powers?" Jason asks redundantly knowing Sabrina wouldn't have the answer. "Wake him!" With Jason's command Rein gives a solid right hook pounding the consciousness into him.

"Ow, what the f-"

"Where is this base!?" Jason's yells as O wakes up.

"Where's what? Where am I!?" Osiris says confused and in pain.

Jason grips O's neck leaning in real close. "I'm asking the questions," He says sternly; irritable.

"What're you gonna do, kiss me?" O mocks at how close Jason is to his face. Jason lets go and steps back allowing for Rein to close in with five knuckles to O's abdomen.

"Where's your second persona!?" Jason asks.

"My second what?" O replies queuing Rein to give him another fist to the right side of his ribs. O let's out a wail then responds to the pain. "What're you talking about!?"

"Your second persona! The thing that gives you powers!? Are you using pills!?" Jason yells. "Sabrina, keep on him! Make sure he's not lying." Sabrina just nods.

"Persona? Pills?" O says looking up, then turns his attention toward Rein. "What have you told him?" Rein replies by clocking him in the face with the blunt end of his elbow.

"Shut up and tell us how you are able to use your powers!" Rein yells in his face.

"It's not pills." Osiris says spitting blood to the floor. "It's not this second person you speak of. It's much more complicated than that."

"What is it?" Jason asks.

"Even if I tell you, what do you get out of it?"

"Information," Jason replies.

"And what would you do with this information? What could you possibly hope to achieve?" O questions.

"That's none of your business, now tell us before Rein decides to knock you around some more."

O looks at Rein, noticing as his own blood drips from the tips of Rein's knuckles. "It's not the pills they were feeding Rein nor this Persona you were talking about."

"Continue," Rein barks.

"Rogue One," Osiris scoffs. "L's play thing."

"I'm no one's play thing,'" Jason says looking away, "Not anymore."

"It's some kind of drug, not pills… It involves needles," Sabrina says; eyes closed, two fingers on the temple of her head and her other hand palm up in O's direction.

"Yes. We found a more efficient way of supplementing the drug using liquid rather than pills. Stays in the human body's system longer," O confesses.

"And the base? This laboratory of yours. Where is it?" Jason asks calmly.

"That... I'm not telling you that," Osiris replies earning him Rein's fist against his cheek bone.

"Maybe you'd like a taste of your own medicine, huh?" Rein says lifting his knuckles to his mouth licking the blood.

"Have fun," Osiris says with a smile. Rein holds out his hand trying to conjure electricity in his palm. To his surprise nothing is happening. "I don't have my powers right now. The solution has already left my system."

"He's right. This solution injected via needles can only stay inside for about five hours," Sabrina says retaining her position. "At least that's what I'm finding in his head."

"It's been a little less than twenty-four," Jason says walking over to Osiris. "L. Where is she?"

"She's relaxing with her feet up at our base comfortably. You won't find her."

"Like hell I won't. You working for her? What does she want with me now?" O just laughs in reply. "Amusing?"

"Very! You know nothing, do you?"

"I know she's using guys with abilities, and I know I need to stop her," Jason growls.

"Good luck with that, Pal."

Sabrina, he's not going to tell us anything. I say we try something else. Jason thinks knowing Sabrina will pick up on his thoughts.

What do you suggest? she thinks back.

"We'll be back. I hope you have some answers for us or you'll taste more of Rein's fists," Jason says, walking toward the exit while Rein and Sabrina follow suit.

"What's your plan?" Sabrina asks back inside the mansion.

"Rein, you were on the streets for a while, right? Do you have any connections?" Jason asks.

"What kind of connections?" he asks.

"We need drugs. Something to throw his focus off, at least until Sabrina can fish out some information."

"Yeah, I'll see what I can do. Let me wash off and I'll head out right away," Rein says walking off.

"Sabrina, I want you to go with him since he can't manipulate any powers right now." Sabrina nods. "And pick up his stuff while you're out. If he's going to be a part of this, he can't be living under a bridge," Jason adds.

"I'd be more than happy to," She says as she turns to walk away. "What're you going to do?" she says before taking a step.

"I'm going to train some more. I have a feeling after this, we're going to have a fight on our hands." Jason soon disappears around the corner and down the hallway.

Rein and Sabrina hop in her red Jeep and head out of the mansion gates.

"L. Who is she?" Rein asks.

"That's a long story," Sabrina replies without diverting her head from the road.

"I'm sure we've got time," Rein insists holding out his hand. "Let me borrow your phone." Rein takes the phone and starts sending out text messages left and right.

"She's Jason's ex-girlfriend, and she's had supernatural abilities like you, Jason and me."

"So what? They were in the same laboratory they kept me in and hooked up later?"

"No," Sabrina, keeping her concentration on the road, almost going into a daze of memories "They were together before any of this started. Two years to be exact."

"Two couples with super powers? Damn, they must have a lot of fun," Rein says sounding astonished.

"Actually L had powers and was using them to control Jason. See she has the ability to control the chemicals in another person's body and make them think they are in love with them. If she concentrated her powers she could actually make them feel anything she wants since emotions are merely just chemical balances and imbalances in the body."

Rein's face still aimed at Sabrina's phone as he shoots out message after message trying to find one of the local drug dealers responds "So how did they get their powers, and why didn't Jason realize that he was under her powers?"

"Well, Jason doesn't know how he, nor L gained their powers, but after they broke up he and I met each other in a crazy car accident." She looks up into the sky, the blue and pink hues over them. "He saved my life that night."

During the ride Sabrina explains to Rein how he ripped the door off her car and raced her to the emergency room. How she got his phone number from reading his mind the night he visited her, their meeting up downtown and Jason seeing L that same night at the club.

"After that we kept in touch, had lunch every now and then. Jason told me about his relationship with her and how it all made sense when I told him about her powers."

"Damn, sounds like a lot went down six months ago," Rein says.

"Yeah, it was all pretty dramatic. Ever since then we haven't seen her. I guess from the intel Jason's received she's moved out of her mom's house and is now living with some guy. Nobody knows where that is exactly, but Jason is determined to find her and stop her."

"Stop her? What's she doing that's so bad?"

"What if you ran into her, and she put you under the same spell?" Sabrina begins to explain as she turns off the freeway onto the Fourth Street exit. "What if she was able to make you do whatever she wanted you to do? You two run into someone else with abilities like ours and you take control of them." Sabrina's Jeep comes to a halt at the stop light nearing the end of the exit ramp. "What if you took control of their powers and she made you rob a bank, or steal a car or worse... kill somebody?"

"Yeah, I can see your point, but she never made Jason do any of that right?" Rein asks innocently.

"Well, no, but there was always the possibility. Jason can control his adrenaline system giving him enlarged muscles which could have countless possibilities. We don't want her having control over someone like that."

"Turn right," Rein says just before the light turns green. "Yeah, I guess I see what you're saying. If she had control over any of the people at the lab I was confined in, that would be bad. Well... depending on what kind of person she is anyway."

"She left Jason for someone else, that should tell you enough of what kind of person she is," Sabrina scowls.

"Yeah, but if she could control him and use his powers just like that, why didn't she continue? Did Jason actually rob a bank or hurt anybody?"

"Not that he's spoken of, but someone with those powers can't be left unchecked."

"Alright, make a left here and turn down the first alleyway," Rein says softly. "Then why what would make you think she would actually do something like that to someone else?"

"Listen, Jason wants her stopped and put in check and that's what we're going to do. She may have abilities and use them however she wants, but so do we and we need to use them for the greater good." She makes the turn down the alleyway he spoke of bringing the Jeep to stop. "Or at least not use them for evil."

"What makes you think she's going to use her powers for evil?" Rein asks.

"The point is, she can control someone's emotions and that's wrong. End of story."

"You can read peoples minds, levitate objects with your mind and who knows what else. What makes you think the same can't be said about you?"

"Look, someone's coming," Sabrina says dodging the questions. Rein picks up on her being so dodgy, leaving it alone knowing you need to pick and choose your battles.

Rein doesn't know where L's allegiances lie, but he does know that bringing down the laboratory he was trapped in for a year is number one priority and if it leads Sabrina and Jason to L, then their goals are mutual.

Ripped, blue jeans are revealed in the headlights of Sabrina's Jeep. As he draws closer his upper body is slowly revealing a dark hoodie and only a beard visibly draping down from underneath his hood.

"I need some cash," Rein says stepping into the alleyway out of the Jeep. Sabrina slips him a hundred dollar bill. "I won't need this much." Sabrina shrugs. Rein shuts the door and proceeds to meet the hooded man between the headlights as though they're given a spotlight. A few minutes go by before Rein returns to Sabrina's passenger seat.

"What did you get?" Sabrina asks curiously; cautiously.

"I got a little bit of the C," Rein says slipping the baggy of white powder into the glove compartment. "Don't you worry your pretty little rich butt. It's only drugs." Sabrina looks forward as the hooded man disappears around the corner. She takes a big gulp and shifts the Jeep into reverse bringing her back to the street.

"Let's go get your stuff."

"Oh, yeah, here's your change," Rein says handing Sabrina two twenty's back. "By the way, the estate you're living in, how could you possibly afford that by yourself at your age?"

"It was my parents to be honest. My brother and I only inherited the mansion through their will along with their corporate empire," Sabrina explains hopping onto the freeway. "The company pretty much runs itself with multiple branching companies. Sinclair industries."

"Sinclair industries? I'm sure I've heard of that somewhere," Rein says placing one finger to his chin pondering hard.

"Most likely, we've got plenty of different industries out there so if one is going under or losing profits, we can always count on the others to pull it back up."

"I'm not talking about seeing it while shopping or in a commercial. I mean I've seen that name somewhere recently," Rein urges.

Sabrina pulls off the freeway heading onto a frontage road heading down a dead end. "Maybe at my place today?" The Jeep pulls in front a road block sign placing it in park killing the lights. The two get out heading to the underside of the bridge.

"No, no, no, I've seen it before I met you and Jason. I'm sure of it."

Under the bridge Sabrina and Rein begin gathering Rein's essentials like his clothes, what little money he has stashed and his scattered cans of food. Rein is gathering up his sleeping bag and shoving his stuff into different bags he's collected since he escaped the laboratory. "That's it!" Rein yells dropping one of his bags to the floor giving a loud thud.

"What is it!?" Sabrina exclaims turning around.

"I know where I've seen Sinclair Industries!"

Sabrina just remains silent waiting for an answer.

"Your company's logo was everywhere at the laboratory I was confined in."

Chapter Nine

He hacks and slashes, he dives and leaps; Jason trains vigorously, sweat dripping from his brow and like a snake slithers on its body so does the drops of liquid down his etched body. "That's work kid." Jason turns around, blade drawn to the sudden voice. His guard drops noticing it's only Sabrina's older brother Christós standing in the doorway.

"Yeah, it's a daily routine," Jason replies placing his blade within its scabbard. "You snuck up on me. When did you get back anyway?"

"Long enough to see you can run up a wall flawlessly," Christós says with a scoff.

"Does that bother you?" Jason swings a towel over the back of his neck patting his face off as he walks toward Christós, but he just looks away. "Anyway, Sabrina said something came up at your work?"

"Yeah, turns out one my employees decided to take a leave of absence in the middle of his work," Jason walks right past him and down the hallway. Christós follows.

"That sucks. Will it affect your work?"

"He was one of my best. Either way, everyone is replaceable." The corridors of the mansion dark, only being illuminated by the small candles lit. "How 'bout a drink?"

"I don't really-"

"I insist." Christós says taking lead in their trek down the dimly lit hallway.

"Sure, why not."

Christós grabs two bottles of beer out of Sabrina's stainless steel refrigerator. He closes the fridge as he turns around and takes his place next to Jason on the granite island. "Tell me about yourself, Jason."

"What's there to tell?" Jason replies popping open the bottle with a twist.

"Let's start with your relationship with my little sister."

"We're friends, that's all really," Jason takes a drink.

Christós follows suit. "My sister is beautiful, smart and has inherited a fortune. You can't tell me that you don't have any interest in her."

Placing the drink on the table, Jason looks down. The strands of his black hair fall over his face. "To be completely honest, I don't have an interest in relationships right now."

"Hmm?"

"I've got unfinished business I need to take care of before I can pursue anything else," Jason grips the bottle tightly in the palm of his hands.

"What kind of business?" Christós asks curiously.

"This girl I used to know. I need closure. I need to know…" He stops for a second, but before he can continue with his thought the door creaks open.

"Jason? Christós?" Sabrina calls out.

"In the kitchen little sister," Christós calls out. Sabrina enters but stops the moment her eyes catch glimpse of the two sitting together.

"What's going on?" she asks cautiously.

"Your friend, Jason, and I are just chitchatting."

"Hey, where can I put my stuff?" Rein says revealing himself behind Sabrina.

"There's just boys popping up everywhere!" Christós spews out sarcastically.

"Uhh, Christós, I'd like to introduce you to my other friend. His name is Rein." Looking back at Rein she continues her polite etiquette. "Rein, this is my brother, Christós."

It's, umm, nice to meet you, sir," Rein says still holding his box of stuff.

"Sir? Please, don't patronize me," Christós says with a smile. "I'm not even in my thirties yet." He laughs. "Jason, if you'll excuse me." Jason only nods his head. Christós walks away nudging Sabrina as he passes her. "Rein, you can put your stuff upstairs in the bedroom down the left hallway. It's the fourth door on the right." He turns his head around to catch Jason in his vision. "That's next to your room if I'm correct." Jason nods once more. "Alright then, Sabrina." Slowly he disappears around the corner. Sabrina follows.

Following him some ways to the study Christós takes a seat at an old, dusty writing desk made of wood. Sabrina takes her place in front. "Yes, brother?"

"You're not being wise, little sister," Christós says folding the fingers of his hands together.

"You can trust them, I promise. You saw the way Jason came to my rescue when you came home that night."

"Yes, and I also have seen the survival instincts he possesses. Do you even know these guys?" He lowers his head so that his mouth is hidden behind his hands. "How do you know they're not just taking advantage of you?"

"We share a mutual goal," She says looking away fixating her gaze on an old bookcase. The same bookcase her mother used to pull books from as she read to Sabrina in the past.

"I know it's hard living in this big home without them, but you can't just bring random people in here," he says sympathetically.

"Maybe if you were around more, I wouldn't be so lonely!" Sabrina yells. She takes a step back covering her mouth realizing that this was the first time she's ever raised her voice to Christós. She turns, running out the door. Stopping around the corner, Sabrina places two fingers to her head hoping to hear Christós' thoughts on the matter. *What the?* She thinks to herself. *I can't hear anything.*

"*Sabrina, is everything okay?*" Jason asks using only his thoughts.

She lowers her hands from her face looking up searching for him. Slowly he steps out of a shadow. "*Yeah, we're fine. I just need a drink,*" She says telepathically as she walks past him. "*Where's Rein?*"

"*He's upstairs putting his stuff away,* He replies following her back into the kitchen. "Did you two grab the stuff?" he asks sitting down.

"Yeah. When are we doing this?" Sabrina asks in reply.

"We'll have to do it after your brother has left. We can't risk him finding out about us."

"Good idea," Sabrina says cracking open a beer.

The midnight hour falls while Jason, Sabrina and Rein congregate in the kitchen over a couple of Blue Moon beers communicating telepathically as well as verbally as to not raise any sort of suspicion of Christós.

It's getting late, I'm guessing your brother is going to stay in tonight? Rein asks telepathically.

"There's no way Captain America could beat Spider-Man in a fight!" Sabrina says. *Yeah, that's what I'm thinking,* she adds telepathically.

"Captain America has the same strength as Spider-Man, but he has all the training of a soldier. You just can't argue with that." Rein replies. Then silently, *Alright, after he falls asleep then.* "What do you do think, Jason?"

After he falls asleep is good, but someone is going to need to keep a look out to make sure he doesn't wake up, Jason replies. Rein and Sabrina stare at him with angst. Jason conjures a look of confusion then quickly snaps, "There's no way either of them could beat Nightcrawler!" Sabrina and Rein hysterically laugh out of control. "What?" Jason asks confused once more.

"Nightcrawler!? No way! He has no super strength or reflexes! All he can do is teleport!" Rein says pointing out the obvious.

"Whatever, I bet out of all the X-Men you would choose Rogue, and let's not forget that teleportation is a very useful ability! Right, Rein?"

"Now what if you could combine every one of those abilities into one person hmm?" Christós says entering the conversation. "Wouldn't that be something marvelous?"

"Now that would be amazing, but I think that if that were to happen, it would put a huge strain on the body having so many abilities, and no way to sort through them at will," Jason says taking a sip of his beer.

"Exactly!" Christós says taking a seat next to Sabrina who sits across from Jason. "What if you could extract each one of these powers into some kind of pill or liquid drink and ingest them whenever you'd like!? You could choose which abilities to use when and where you choose without straining the body!"

"I'm sure that's not so far fetched as someone would think," the confusion in Rein's voice becomes very apparent.

Christós scoots back in his chair rising to his feet. "Well, I'm off to bed, kids. Don't stay up too late, it's a school night after all," Christós says exiting the room.

"But none of us are even in school," Rein adds quickly.

"That was a joke, Rein," Jason responds in correction.

"I knew that!" Rein answered. "I was joking too."

"Right," Patronization written all over Sabrina's reply.

Christós' footsteps quietly dissipate up the stairs into silence. The odd trio with their beers wait another hour to make sure Christós has fallen asleep before they make their way out to the Sabrina's backyard and back down to the basement.

"Rein, I think you should stay inside the house and make sure Christós doesn't wake up," Jason says as they walk down into the dark.

"Alright, I'm fine with that, but I need you to question O about Sinclair Industries," Rein asks just before heading out.

"Sinclair Industries? What're you talking about?"

"Sabrina can fill you in," Rein says as he shuts the door behind them.

"Rein said he saw my companies logo in the institute where he was locked away, but I don't know if it actually has anything to do with my family or just a rogue branch. I can't exactly oversee everything that goes on."

"Maybe you should work on looking into your business a bit more. What if you've hired L and you don't even know it," Jason said scornfully.

"I wouldn't hire someone like that, Jason! Plus I would need to know her name in order for me to hire her and I don't even hire anyone!" Sabrina's flurried voice reached down the stairs to O still strapped to a chair.

"You two argue like a married couple," He said as Jason and Sabrina approached.

"Yeah, and we're about to squeeze info outta you like a married couple would to a child," Jason says cracking his knuckles.

"Then you shouldn't ever have kids if you're going to abuse them like you do me." Jason collides his knuckles against O's jaw halting his sentence sending blood across the room. O jerks his head back popping his neck. "You see, that's what I'm ta-" Jason punches him once again this time cutting him off.

"Jason…" Sabrina says behind him.

"Fine," He says backing off.

Jason continued interrogating Osiris with less violence making sure not to upset Sabrina. Osiris, like a vault, didn't let anything valuable slip due to Jason's fists. Like any good thief though, Jason and Sabrina were prepared to crack the safe and take what they needed. With a flick of a wrist, Sabrina pulled out a small bag of white powder handing it Jason. "Do you know what this is?" he asks holding it up to O's face as the blood drips down the side of his cheek. "It's cocaine. You like taking drugs, right? These vials of solution that give you power over electricity. Well, let's try something a little more… street, shall we?"

Jason pours a bit of the white powder onto his left hand, sets the bag down and with his left he takes hold of O's head from the back. He shoves O's head into the palm of his hand where the powder sits forcing Osiris to inhale all the powder at once. "Now, let's see how cooperative you are with a small dosage, hmmm?" Jason pulls up a nearby seat plotting himself down comfortably and very calmly asks, "Where is this laboratory that Rein was experimented on?"

Osiris's pupils become pinned as he stares at intently as Jason, "I ain't telling you jack shit!" Osiris replies spitting onto the ground. "You think just cause you get me high that I'll spill the information?"

"Like a broken glass of water, my friend," Jason replies. "Now I'm going to ask you again. Where is this lab?"

"You can keep trying, I'm still not saying anything to you."

"I'll take your advice then," Jason gets up forcing more cocaine down O's nostrils. "Ready to talk?"

Osiris's pupils decrease even more, his hands begin to fidget, and his breathing becomes quicker. "I'm just getting high, it's not like it's a truth serum."

"This lab… You were there, right?" O gives no response. "Your boss, L, is there too huh?" Still, O remains silent. "And you were there when Rein was there. Did you send him to bait us?"

Keep going. You're starting to make him think. Sabrina says telepathically.

"L told you about me. That's why you came after me. She knows that I'm looking for her." O lets out a small laugh causing Jason to thrust his fist across O's face causing blood to spew out. "Don't you mock me!"

"Jason!" Sabrina says sternly making Jason stand up straight cracking his neck as he takes a deep breath. "Just stay calm."

"Now tell me. Where is L and her laboratory? What is she planning on doing there?"

"Jason, you've got it all wrong. You think this is about you?" Osiris spits again letting out a chuckle then looks back up at him. "You will never find where the lab is."

"Got it!" Sabrina shouts. "We didn't expect you to tell us outright, but we knew that if we broke your concentration with drugs, you wouldn't be able to keep your mind focused."

"Smart, but that's all you're getting out of me, Jason." As O says these words the objects in the room begin to levitate. O's chair slowly lifts off the ground just as both Sabrina and Jason do. The tables around them, the tools and everything else scattered about the cellar rise off the ground just floating in midair. "My buddies have just arrived."

Out of thin air, Jason is kicked in the chest sending him floating across the room and into the wall behind him. "What the hell!?" Suddenly his foot is grabbed and soon he's swung around and being let go, casing him into Sabrina, slamming them both to one side of the room.

"Took you long enough!" O says causing a girl to materialize out of thin air. Short blonde hair streaked with black strands reaching just below the height of her chin. The black tank top she's sporting barely covers anything allowing the tops of her breasts to protrude obviously while her black miniskirt almost reaches mid-thigh level, but the combat boot stretching just below her knees don't do much to help."Don't count on her fighting fair, you won't be able to see her much longer."

"It's nice to meet you two, but I'm not alone," Katerina says as a man draped in a cloak walks down the cellar stairs. "His name is Castiel, he's the one causing the zero gravity in the room." No physical features can be seen about Castiel due to the dark cloak covering his entire body except the long strands of blond hair hanging from his oversized hood. "Don't worry about his apparel, he just has a flare for the dramatics," Katerina says untying the ropes that bind O to his chair. "We'll be taking our friend here, and you two will be dying now,"

Katerina adds on with a giggle in her voice and a wink in her eye. "Castiel, crush them!" Castiel's arm raises out of the cloak with his palm reaching in their direction. He slowly closes his fingers increasing the gravity around them with every inch.

The weight of Castiel's gravity is the form of an orb with Jason and Sabrina floating in the middle. With the gravity increasing, their bodies mesh together more and more which would eventually flatten their bodies against one another until the point they both end. "Sabrina! Do something!" Jason shouts

"Like what!?" Sabrina replies hastily.

"I don't know, use your telepathic powers to... augh!" he shouts, "to stop him or something!" Sabrina looks around the room noticing nothing else is being crushed under the weight of Castiel's gravity. *I wonder if I can do the same thing with my power, kinda like I did with the water the other night.* Sabrina's thoughts begin to manifest with her power creating an orb around Jason and herself. This visible orb proceeds to push back the gravitational push against their bodies. "Whatever you're doing, Sabrina, it's working!"

"What the hell, Castiel!? Crush them!" Katerina yells out, frustrated picking Osiris up off the chair. Castiel just lets out a grunt in reply, rapidly closing his hand into fist. Sabrina's orb starts to shrink around them once again.

"Jason, I can't hold it!" Sabrina yells out.

"You can do it, just keep your concentration up!" The orb becomes smaller and smaller with every second passing by. Jason and Sabrina's bodies once again are pressed up against each other. The weight of the gravity becomes crushingly apparent with the pain increasing.

"Jason, is this it?" Sabrina asks, starting to cry with the idea of death becoming a reality.

"No, just hold on, Sabrina!" As the words leave his lips Rein storms down the stairs wielding one of Jason's swords, swinging it erratically. "Rein?" Jason says to himself. Castiel loses concentration by Rein's radical behavior dropping the gravity field around Jason and Sabrina, letting both fall to the ground. Castiel increases the gravity on Rein substantially slamming his body to the ground making him fumble the blade in his hand and pinning him to the ground. Blood slowly leaks from underneath his head. "Sabrina, are you okay?" Jason asks helping her up. "I think so, but what about Rein?" Jason turns his attention toward Rein seeing him being crushed under the weight of the gravity Castiel is creating. Quickly, Jason darts in Castiel's direction, scooping up his sword on the way, thrusting the blade toward his neck, but much to Jason's surprise, the sword is deflected by a floating lead pipe, but he rapidly follows up his attack with another swing slicing the pipe in half. Using his momentum, his body follows the path of his sword spinning around and after making a full 180 degree turn, he lets out a backward kick filled with concentrated adrenaline hitting an invisible Katerina with the power of a fully grown horse into the cloak of Castiel. They both plummet to the floor as Jason squares himself up to stand over both of the fallen enemies. "Did L send you?"

"You still don't know anything, Jason!" O laughs lying on the ground near the back of the cellar but just as Jason looks up, he's blasted back by a bolt of lightening. Jason loses consciousness after gaining severe burns on his chest with small hints of smoke rising. Castiel and Katerina picked themselves the ground slowly heading up the stairs with O over each of their arms. "We need to tell the boss to be ready for an attack," O whispers to his comrades just before disappearing outside.

Chapter Ten

No lights are on, only Sabrina's laptop screen illuminating the basement infirmary. The only sounds echoing below her mansion are the keys clicking underneath her fingertips as she researches the information found inside Osiris's head hours ago. Jason and Rein lay on separate operating beds injured and unconsciousness. Sabrina patched them both up as best she could, but as there were no open flesh wounds she could only bind them.

Before the altercation with Katerina and Castiel, Sabrina managed to find out the street the laboratory was located on. While probing his head as Jason interrogated O being on drugs, Osiris thought about heading back to the lab after he made his escape which lead him to think about the street called Jefferson. Jefferson Street, an unlikely place for a laboratory to be kept. Although when she looked up nearby laboratories on Jefferson, she could only find a community economic laboratory which didn't deal with human experiments. Although who would really list that under their research projects in their Google Maps profile? No, Sabrina remembered that Rein saw the Sinclair logo while he was there and her company had nothing to do with the other economic research labs on Jefferson Street.

As she researched she found a toy store located on Jefferson street that was owned by her family. Sinclair Toys and Gadgets. *I don't get it,* Sabrina thought to herself, *Jefferson Street. Sinclair Toys and an economic lab? This doesn't make much sense.* She scratched the temples of her head under the laptop's light with great confusion swirling inside.

Sabrina, don't you think you should get some rest? Shae advised as a thought inside.

I have to figure this out, Jason is depending on me, Sabrina urges pulling up another folder in her companies files. *I know I can find this lab.*

All you have is a street name, nothing more, Shae makes the obvious even more apparent.

And with Osiris gone and my home on the enemie's radar, I HAVE to find it. Sabrina flips in and out of folders left and right 'til she comes across Sinclair Toys. *I think I've found something!*

What is it? Shae asks.

It's the blueprints for this business. There's something strange about it though. Sabrina clicks and scrolls through the prints looking at every corner realizing there's something off about it. *There's this shaft in the back. It leads down about thirty feet underground and then just stops.*

That's strange, do you think this could be it? Shae probes Sabrina's reasoning.

I think it's worth checking out, Sabrina says confidently plugging in her USB Flash Drive.

Sabrina's room is uniquely set up so that when the sun rises, it's light is captured by a single window facing toward the east lined with tiny reflecting mirrors intensifying the light and casting it upon the pillows of Sabrina's bed forcing her to wake up with the day. The light triggers Sabrina's consciousness to peel back the lids of her eyes. She groans picking herself up into a sitting position. Hands like weights, she struggles in raising them to her face to clear the sleeping sand from her eyes. "Sabrina, I'm heading out!" Christós shouts from downstairs snapping Sabrina's eyes wide open. She leaps out of bed and straight to the door without ever touching ground. The door swings right open allowing her to hover just inches off the ground in a quickened pace to the staircase. She finally arrives at the banister atop the stairs only to catch a glimpse of Christós's back slipping out the front door. "Bye, brother..." She whispers knowing he wouldn't hear her.

Where is he off to in such a hurry? Shae asks from inside.

"I have no idea," Sabrina says blankly. "I should check on the boys." Without delay she hops on over the railings hovering to the bottom gracefully then tiptoeing across the cold hardwood floors. She quietly makes her way down the metal spiral stairs only to find both Jason and Rein are still out like a light. "Aren't they adorable?" Sabrina awes at the sight of the two bandaged boys.

I hardly think that's the right word for them.

"Oh, hush, Shae, let's go make breakfast for when they wake up!" Sabrina says with excitement hovering back up the stairs and into the kitchen. "Hmmm, what to make? Pancakes? Omelettes? Eggs and Bacon? Or what about Bacon Pancakes?"

All of that sounds lovely, Sabrina!

"Then I'll make all of it."

Suddenly food flies out of the closet pantry, the fridge, spices out of the cabinet atop the microwave mounted on the wall, dishes swirling. The kitchen is drenched in chaos with everything swirling around in a tornado of food, pots, pans along with everything else in the kitchen. Eggs begin to break open, the stove ignites, cooking oil sprays out of it's container splashing onto a mid-air frying pan coming to rest upon the stove as the eggs plop themselves in the oil. While the eggs cook, potatoes fall from the whirlwind in the kitchen onto the granite counters with kitchen knives slicing and dicing them into perfect little squares. A powder of pancake fog mixes together with water above Sabrina's head, swirling around inside what seems to be an invisible bubble growing more and more thick into a cooking batter eventually separating into individual saucers.

With a flick of her wrist, Sabrina brings out the griddle allowing the pancake saucers to safely land atop the griddle as it heats up. The potatoes come to rest into a giant wok with different spices and ingredients coming together as seasoning. Last but not least, the bacon is shoved into the oven after a period of preheating. Sabrina takes a look around noticing everything she wants cooked is currently cooking so she calms the whirlwind sending everything back to where it belongs slowly and neatly. *That wasn't so hard was it?* Sabrina thinks to Shae.

You've impressed me once again Sabrina! Managing to use your abilities as you wish and this time without having to break the barrier between you and I!

"Thank you Shae!" Sabrina says placing a huge grin upon her face.

Just don't burn the food.

"Hey! I'm a very good cook! I can cook with two hands tied behind my back!" Sabrina exclaims in her defense.

The entire cooking process takes about an hour for everything to be cooked to Sabrina's level of satisfaction and delicious perfection. She sorts the food into three different portions guessing Christós isn't going to come back anytime soon. The aroma fills the kitchen with the sweet scent of bacon that would wake up the deepest slumberer. Taking in a big whiff she lets out a sigh of relief then proceeds downstairs into the infirmary. Jason and Rein lay motionless upon their respective operating tables making less than a sound. Sabrina shakes Jason a little, "Jason, wake up. Food's ready," but she gets no response from him. She turns her attention toward Rein enacting the same technique, but she has even less luck with him. "Damn, these two must be exhausted."

Why don't you try waking them up mentally? Shae advises.

"Mentally?"

Yeah, dive inside their heads and tell them to wake up or something. If you trigger their subconscious mind, you can do it. You read it in a book somewhere if I remember correctly.

"I guess it's worth a shot," Sabrina says dragging her hand along the bed sliding onto Rein's forehead. She brings her other hand up placing both on the sides of his head. "Alright, let's see if I can do this." Closing her eyes she creates a visual of a door leading into Rein's mind and slowly enters. What happens next leaves her completely unprepared.

The doorway leads to a dark corridor with flickering lights. The air is thin and shallow. Her breaths become short and scarce. "Is this the inside of Rein's mind?" A cold breeze whirls by whipping her hair up entangling herself. As she works to escape the trappings she hears a faint scream down one corridor. "What the hell was that!?" She quickens her pace pulling the hair back into a pony tail to deter anymore traps by the wind. "I think it came this way." She slowly takes a step down the corridor readying herself for anything. Each step she takes seems as though it's getting her nowhere. No end to this corridor whatsoever, just miles and miles of the same flickering lights, metal doors, and groaning noises. The atmosphere sends chills down Sabrina's spine and flicking her hair to stand on end.

"These hallways never end, Shae!" Sabrina exclaims in exasperation. Placing one hand on the wall she lets her body lean up against it to take a breather. "Shae, what do I do to wake Rein up if I can't even find him?" She straightens her body upright curiously. "Shae?" But still no response. "What the hell? Where is she?" Sabrina closes her eyes placing two fingers to the side of her head concentrating on finding her, but it's of no use, Shae is completely out of contact. "Why can't I communicate with her, damn it… Because I'm in Rein's mind? It doesn't matter. I can't get hold of her, and I need to find Rein." She continues walking down the corridor with no avail. The doors are all still the same, the lights in the hall still flicker, but now there's an echoing groan coming from behind the metal doors seemingly in synch.

Curiously, Sabrina cracks open one of the heavy metal doors halting the groaning within. Slowly the door creeps open, squealing the whole way through, with a young boy inside. Sabrina steadily steps into the dark room examining the kid. A white rag, ripped and tattered, is all he has for clothing. Leather straps keep him immobilized. Some kind of black cloth is lodged between his teeth tied around the backside of his head.

His hair so long it covers his face like a veil. "Oh, my god!" Sabrina says in a whisper rushing to his side. "Who did this to you?" she asks continuing in her whisper. The boy replies with only a grumble following a mumble. "Oh, let me take that off for you," Sabrina says. She clears the veiled hair away from his face letting out a shout of fear from her voice. The walls begin melting away, floors disappear as reality sets in. Behind the veil is revealed to be a tied up Rein.

"What the hell was that?" Sabrina says coming back to reality.

What was what? Shae questions,

"Oh Shae, you're back!" Sabrina says in exclamation.

Back? But I never… Before Shae can finish Rein begins to wake up from his slumber.

"Oh, my head," He says groggily from the slumber. "How long was I out?"

"A little over nine hours, not too bad for someone who was crushed under heaps of gravity," Sabrina says with a smile.

"Nine hours? Damn, I usually only sleep- augh!" Rein tries getting up but the pain keeps him flat on his back.

"Don't try to move. Your muscles tore pretty badly," Sabrina advises walking over to Jason. "Just rest a little, I'm going to wake this one up now." She places her hands on the sides of his head shutting her eyes slowly. *Shae, I'll be back.*

What do you mean? Just as Shae asks, Sabrina's consciousness is gone inside Jason.

There are birds chirping, rustling in the trees above, scurrying in the bushes, bright rays of sunlight seep through the cracks between the leaves dancing upon the air on their way to the ground. Sabrina's eyes adjust to the bright sight of a vibrant forest full of color, animals, and an orchestrated rhythm of sounds forged from the forest itself. "Is this the inside of Jason's mind?" Sabrina asks herself in awe of her surroundings. "It's all so gorgeous!" There are deer, antelope, and zebra brustling back and forth leaping about. Tigers, lions, panthers, wolves, foxes all run about between trees, although none show any predatory interest in Sabrina. Just as well, Sabrina begins her descent in the forest.

"This is much better than being inside Rein's head; that was scary," Sabrina whispers as though someone is listening. "But where is Jason? Don't tell me he's some sort of Tarzan in a loin cloth!" She laughs at the thought but the laughter slowly quiets as she ponders the sight of Jason wearing nothing but a patch of fabric. A few minutes of daydreaming pass before a small monkey snaps her out of it. Tugging on her hair laughing, or what would be a monkey's laugh, the little creature climbs up a vine it's hanging from. "Hey you! That wasn't very nice!" The monkey squeals back hopping off into the forest out of sight. "What a strange place this is."

Through some bushes she spots the monkey hanging from a tree branch swaying back and forth. She rushes quickly after the little creature brushing past bushes, tree branches, twigs and other such things. The monkey turns to stare her down as she draws closer and closer. Just as the monkey becomes within arm's reach, it disappears once more leaving Sabrina with an unusual sight. She's arrived at the edge of the forest. The trees all stop growing as though there's an invisible wall halting their advancement. Even the branches don't grow past this point. The ground is no longer laid out with soft dirt nor grass, but replaced with dirt, sand and dead carnations tumbling along in the shape of dried-up weeds. A single tree stands in the distance, although it's branches are lacking decorations of leaves or colors. The tree itself is blackened and draping, like gravity is much more harsh here in particular. A cloud hangs above this broken symbol of life, leaking out water at an infinite rate.

Sabrina steps onto the desert sand hearing the ground crack below the soles of her shoes. Another, and another. Each step she takes feels like the temperature is increasing at an alarming rate. By the time she arrived at the tree she'll have died of heat stroke, but before her death at the hands of heat, she inches close enough to see two figures underneath the tree. The shadow from the cloud shades the two just enough to conceal their identities from Sabrina. "That's gotta be Jason!" Realizing that it couldn't be anyone else, she rushes toward them entering the perimeter of the rain, unmasking their identity. She's come to find Jason sitting on the ground becoming drenched in the falling rain as a girl holds him close to her. Sabrina kneels down in front of Jason reaching out her hand to grab his. "Don't touch him," the girl says, "he's mine." Looking up Sabrina peers through the strands of hair hiding her face only to realize it's L holding onto him. "Jason?" Sabrina whispers, and suddenly his eyes shoot open catching hers.

"Sabrina?" Jason says from the flat of his back as she's hovering over him. "What're you doing? Why are your hands holding onto my head like that?"

Back in reality and in her own body, she jumps backwards startled at the abrupt change of scenery. "Oh, umm… Sorry, I was just making sure you were okay." She says grabbing onto her arm rubbing it up and down for comfort. *Shae, how long was I gone for this time?*

What're you talking about? Shae responds in confusion.

I was gone inside Jason's mind, did Rein notice? Sabrina persists.

Sabrina, if your consciousness left then I didn't realize it at all. You must have been converted into a brain wave or something. I don't know much about how the brain works, but I know you can have as many as seven dreams a night and your perception is increased.

I wonder if Jason noticed me in there? Sabrina thinks to herself. "So, Jason, Rein, how did you guys sleep?"

"Sleep? We were knocked out cold!" Jason says irritated. "We lost Osiris too, damn it!"

"We may have lost Osiris, but I think I know where they're going," Sabrina replies pepped up.

"You found the lab!?" Rein says jumping into a sitting position.

"I'll tell you guys everything over breakfast." Sabrina gets up starting down the hall. "Well c'mon, the food isn't getting any warmer," She adds with a wink before walking completely off.

Jason and Rein both arrive at the dinner table quickly becoming ensnared by the aroma of food clouding the atmosphere. The eggs catch their nose like a deadman in a noose, the bacon binds them to their chairs as though strapping a man to an electric chair, and the scent of the pancakes entrap them like a fox inside a bear trap.

"Everything looks delicious!" Rein exclaims sitting down taking haste toward the silverware but they dodge his hands by floating into the air above the dinner table. "What the hell!?"

"Have some manners, Rein!" Sabrina says revealing she's the one dangling the silverware above his head. "Now then, bow your heads please."

"Sabrina, I didn't know you were religious," Jason says pulling out his chair taking a seat.

"I'm not, but we're going to need all the help we can get with what we're about to do." The silverware slowly floats down into Rein's hands as his head bows with the others. "Jason, will you do the honors?"

"We haven't talked in a while I know. Probably ever since I met L, but I'm about to see her again and it looks like we'll need your help again. Give me the strength to face her and keep my friends alive with me as well." Jason peeks his eye up seeing both Sabrina and Rein till bowed, eyes shut. "Also, thank you for this delicious food Sabrina has prepared for us. If I didn't know any better, I'd say that we were already in heaven having a feast of the angels!"

"Awe Jason!" Sabrina says mid prayer.

"Also, thank you for bringing me to these two. I never thought I could find such good people despite all the evil in this world," Rein adds.

"Amen," all three say together beginning to ravenously devour the food before them.

After a few minutes of silence among the three only sharing sounds of gulps and chews, Jason slows his eating process. Soon Reina and Sabrina follow suit. "Jason?" Sabrina asks. "Something wrong with the food?"

"No, I'm just thinking." Jason places his fork down. "So what did you find out about the lab?"

"Well, I got the street name out of O right before those two ambushed us, and I did some digging into my company since Rein mentioned that our logo was found at the lab." She takes a drink of coffee, gulping down with anxiousness. "I found where it's located and strange blueprints tucked away deep inside the companies' archives."

"So, the lab is connected to your company? Any idea who is behind it all? Did you find L's name in there anywhere?" Jason asks persistently.

"No, whoever was orchestrating these files made sure to cover their tracks. The user login's and admin changes were all made anonymous. Not only that, but there are so many people employed by Sinclair Industries that trying to figure out which one would take too much time."

"So then what do you propose?" Rein says taking a sip of his coffee.

"We break into the lab ourselves and figure this whole mess out!"

"Alright!" Jason says getting up. "Let's go!" Without another second passing, Jason is quickly placed back in his chair.

"Not so fast cowboy! We need to prep first," Sabrina says deviously tapping her fingers together.

Chapter Eleven

"No! I say we head out right now!" Jason says sliding back his chair as he rises to his feet furiously.

"Jason, you two just had your asses handed to you last night," Sabrina says with a smirk. "Plus we'd be heading in there half cocked if we left right now."

"Plus I haven't even finished my breakfast!" Rein complains.

"No, we have the element of surprise! Katerina and Castiel are running back to the lab with their tails between their legs! They won't expect a counter-attack so quickly!" Jason persists.

"Or they may be ready and waiting for us to launch an attack right away." Sabrina takes a sip of her coffee, keeping the mug in place where her lips are hidden. "Right now I'm the only one who knows where the lab is and if I'm not mistaken..." Sabrina pauses shooting a stare into Jason's eyes. "You can't read minds." Jason sits back down crossing his arms portraying an upset face. "Jason..." Sabrina says sternly, "Finish your breakfast."

"Okay, so prep," Rein begins "what do you suggest?"

"Well, we know they've got O back and we just met Katerina and Castiel." Sabrina counts on one hand. "We've also got those other two Rein.. umm took care of the other day and who knows how many others there are like them at the lab. We just have to be prepared to face anything once we get there."

"Sabrina's right, Jason. I'm as hasty as you are to get down there and figure everything out for ourselves, but we also don't want to lose our lives at the same time," Rein adds in support of Sabrina having a bit of empathy in his voice.

"Yeah, I guess you guys are right." Jason finally agrees humbly. The trio finishes their food quietly each thinking about what they must do in order to prepare themselves. A heaviness enters the room, an inescapable density in the air thickens to a suffocating degree that breathing becomes a feat comparable to moving mountains. Their stomachs rise to their throats losing their appetites while anxiety sprawls out throughout their skin erecting goosebumps infinitely.

Sabrina's words keep reverberating through their heads reminding them their lives aren't what they used to know. They don't live in the same world as everyone else, not even in a parallel world, but within a different universe entirely. Normal lives don't involve secret laboratories, they don't have a second person living inside of them with the threat of losing yourself, normal people don't have these crazy abilities making them targets of secret organizations. They didn't ask for these lives, but it's what they were given and it's what they will make right.

After breakfast Jason heads off into the dojo to polish up his technique, Sabrina says she's going to head into town to pick up a few things that will help her and the boys in their infiltration, and Rein heads down to the cellar behind Sabrina's mansion. In town, Sabrina finds an old gun shop where her father used to shop. Naturally with knowing the owner of the shop through her father, she's given no trouble in purchasing what she needs.

"These sure are a lot of guns for a young lady such as yourself," The gun clerk states ringing up the various weapons.

"Yeah, well, I thought I'd take up a new hobby," Sabrina states smiling as innocently as possible.

"Your father used to love his guns. It's a shame he had them all donated to the police department," The clerk says with regret. "He sure did have a good heart. It's a shame that one of his old weapons was used in that shooting last week that killed one of those criminals."

"Yeah, now I'm wishing he would have just left his guns to us instead of donating them." The register lets out a loud ding. "So how much is it?"

"After taxes, registration and permit fee's... that'll be $22,456.98." The old clerk looks up with his green visor over his head with worry in his eyes. "Cash or Credit?"

"I've brought cash with me today," Sabrina says pulling out a stack of hundreds."

"Just like your father." Hearing the clerks words, Sabrina just smiles back at him.

In Sabrina's cellar, Rein is devising some kind of waist holster for vials of blood. "There, that should do it." He holds before him a leather belt with six cylindrical slots on each side just big enough to fit a vial of blood within. "With this I can have up to twelve vials of blood, that means two vials of six different powers to dispose of." Rein walks over to his small collection. "I've got blood samples from Jason, Sabrina, and Osiris."

The vials of blood were collected and harvested over a period of time after Jason and Sabrina found out about Rein's abilities. Having found out this knowledge of him, they thought it would be a good idea to stockpile blood for him in case he ever needed powers on demand, although they didn't seem to help him against Castiel's gravitational powers. "Alright! Two vials of psycho-abilities, two vials of superhuman strength, and two vials of electro-abilities," Rein sets the six vials within the six slots on the right side of the leather belt. "Six other empty vials for blood harvest On-Site Procurement," he says setting the other six within the remaining slots. "Alright, I think I'm ready."

Rein heads out of the cellar leaving his vial holster underground embracing the suns rays outside. "Damn that feels good." In his serenity he becomes curious as to how Jason is preparing himself. In his curiosity he heads inside trekking in the direction of Jason's training ground passing an elegant flowerbed laid out before the steps leading up to the granite patio right outside Sabrina's back door. Once inside he heads down hallways covered in cherry oak, hallways with expensive works of art hanging high and low up and down the corridors. Once outside the dojo, Rein slowly slides open the traditional Japanese style door.

"If you want to enter, you must remove your shoes," Jason says sitting in the middle of the room, legs crossed, head bowed, eyes closed motionless.

"Umm, yeah, sure," Rein replies removing his shoes, leaving them outside as he enters.

"Now bow yourself in to show your respect to this Place of the Way." Rein does so obediently. Jason rises to his feet bringing his eyes to meet Rein's. "Now, what brings you in here?"

"Honestly..." Rein says in hesitation. "Curiosity."

"That is good. To know anything, one must start with curiosity of the matter." Jason speaks as though he's a spiritual monk who's trained for years. "Come, let your training begin. I will teach you more in this day than you will learn within a year elsewhere." Rein's curiosity sparks even more.

Jason begins to explain his ability of adrenaline and the effects of it. He delves deep into how the chemical adrenaline has the ability to increase it's user's perception ability. With perception comes vision, the speed of one's thought process and their quickened reflexes. Within a state of constant adrenaline, Jason is able to perceive time more quickly, think faster and essentially learn faster than any normal human would. This is how he is able to train his body and mind at a heightened pace. With this knowledge shared with Rein, Jason offers up his blood so Rein may enter this adrenaline induced state of mind to train with Jason on an elevated level.

Jason teaches Rein basic martial arts techniques such as defensive, offensive, evasive, and countering skills. Rein learns quickly from the adrenaline running in through his body and his experiences being captive at the lab having to be pitted against others almost on a daily basis. Jason shows Rein the pressure points on the body, the weakest links between the joints and the easiest way to bend a foe's body parts in directions they shouldn't travel. "Listen, Rein," Jason says, blocking a punch with his forearm then quickly rotating in a circular manner to give himself the advantage. "They call it Martial Arts for a reason." Jason quickly throws Rein off balance using his own momentum against him then driving his body to the ground. "It's an Art which needs to be perfected."

A few hours pass while Jason and Rein train diligently at an accelerated rate infusing knowledge within both of them through experience. While they train, Sabrina is off at a shooting range with her new guns. Holstered to her hips are two Colt Single Action Army hand guns and two SOCOM 1911's resting within her shoulder strap holsters. She stands before the shooting range with two boxes of ammo, one for the Single Action and one for her SOCOM.

Her instructor, an older man of about fifty years old, stands beside her ready to teach her all the skills needed for firing a weapon, but Sabrina has other plans in mind. Sabrina uses her abilities to delve into the brain of her instructor, diligently searching and downloading information from his mind into her own with the reward of gaining all his knowledge on firearms and the techniques in using such weapons. Within a matter of minutes, Sabrina is able to unload a full clip of her SOCOM and the entire six shots of her SAA with a 97% accuracy hit rate.

"That was amazing!" The gun instructor exclaims. "You're the best damn rookie I've seen in a long time!"

"Thank you," Sabrina replies shyly. "Beginner's luck?"

"That was more than just beginner's luck! I've been at this for years, and I've only had an accuracy score a handful of times." The instructor persists, "What's your name?"

"It's Sabrina, Sabrina Sinclair," She answers politely.

"The same Sinclair of Sinclair Industries?"

"Umm.. Yes?"

"Your father, his name was Logan Sinclair. Am I right?"

"Yes, that's right." Sabrina begins to suspect something weird is happening here caught up in this impromptu interrogation. "What's with all the questions?"

"Your father, Logan, he used to come here all the time." The instructor leans back against a nearby wall. "Sorry, I never even told you my name. The names Marty."

"You knew my father?" Sabrina asks dropping the suspicions shifting into curiosity.

"Knew him? Your father was my wingman! We used to compete in marksman tournaments together. He was damn near the best SAA shooter." Marty gives a slight chuckle in his reminiscent thoughts. "It's how he earned his name, Revolver."

Sabrina, standing in shock, has just found out something she never knew about her father. He was a marksman. A damn good one too. How did she not know this? Were there medals in the mansion somewhere she hadn't seen. What else didn't she know about him?

"Revolver, huh?" Sabrina smirks in confidence.

"Yeah. He always preferred using a Revolver for it's lack of jamming. Each shot indivi-"

"dually loaded and fired without worry of jamming," Sabrina finishes Marty's sentence and going on. "Yeah, that's what he used to tell everyone who ever asked him about his choice of gun."

"Yeah, your father was a great man!" He says as Sabrina holsters her guns brushing past him. "Hey, where are you going? Don't you wanna finish up the rest of these rounds?" Sabrina doesn't give an answer, she just slowly walks out of the gun shop. Sabrina's downloaded so much information on her father from Marty's mind she's becoming overwhelmed with all his memories of him. She takes herself to a nearby secluded park searching these newly acquired memories.

"Thank you for training me, Jason," Rein says appreciatively throwing a towel over his shoulders.

"Don't mention it. You'll need it tomorrow when we finally put an end to all of this," Jason replies in a very low, raspy voice. "Anyway, you're more than welcome to continue training, but I'm actually going to head out for a while."

"Yeah, no, I've got something I have to take care of anyway, but I'll see you later tonight." Jason nods in acknowledgement giving Rein exit. Rein is out of sight within seconds and back in the cellar. Jason takes his leave in his two toned car heading out as the sun slowly hides beyond the horizon.

By the time Jason hops up onto the hood of his Scion the sun completely disappears setting the ocean of lights a laze as he gazes into the city at the end of the highway. "Nine Mile Hill. This is where everything moved forward," Jason says in the voice of a defeated fighter. "What happened to us?"

Nine Mile Hill, the place where Jason first pressed his lips against L's, where he took her for his own and the very same place they made love together. This place of serenity used to be his place of escape when he couldn't handle life, but now it leaves a sour taste in his mouth.

"There you go again, being all broody," Jack says manifesting in front of Jason. "L, man, it's what she does. She plays with boys as if they were toys."

"Yeah, but it's still hard to think about it," Jason says lowering his head slightly. "And tomorrow, tomorrow I'm going to confront her face to face."

"You're scared, aren't you?" Jack asks.

"Yeah."

"You don't know what you'll do once you actually see her, huh?"

"No, I don't," Jason replies fearfully.

"You still love her, don't you?" Jack asks empathetically.

"..."

"You don't have to answer."

"After all this time, I didn't know it could still hurt this much, Jack," Jason says completely hiding his face under his arms which are resting on his bent knees.

"You'll finally be able to put this all to rest tomorrow, Jason. Just hang in there."

"Better to have loved and lost than to never have loved at all, right?" Jason asks raising his head toward the stars revealing tears sliding down his face. "I say ignorance is bliss." Jason let's out a sigh of sadness placing a cigarette between his lips as he sets the end ablaze.

"Jason..." Jack says looking on at him with pity. "When are you going to kick those damn cancer sticks?"

He takes a puff and slowly answers with smoke emitting with every word. "When this is all over, my friend... When it's all over." Jason hops off the hood of his car slowly rounding toward the driver side door. Jason takes one more puff of his cigarette tossing the stick away. Letting out the last of his smoke he opens the door and turning toward Jack, "Oh, and to answer your question. Yes, I do still love L." Jack ignited the two-toned Scion with an intense rev of the engine as he sped off back toward the mansion.

Coincidentally Jason arrives back at the mansion at the same time as Sabrina pulls in simultaneously parking. Engines killed, lights out and doors open. "Where are you coming from?" Sabrina asks.

"Nowhere special, just trying to clear my head before tomorrow," Jason says rounding his vehicle in a very low voice.

"Are you ready for this?"

"As ready as I'll ever be." Jason walks past Sabrina straight inside the mansion finding Rein waiting for him. "Rein?"

"I hope you don't mind." He says pulling Jason's sword from behind his back. "I've made some modification to your blade."

"What kind of modifications?" Jason asks with a suspicious look.

The once traditional blade now has a hollow look to it. The blade, now serrated, is filtered with a single hollowed out tunnel running through the blade down to the tsuba and into the handle which also has a slight hollowing capsule. At the end of the hilt lies an intravenous tube running within the handle's capsule. The intravenous tube is encased inside a leather, buckle fastened wrist strap which ultimately would be inserted via vein.

"Rein, what have you done to my sword?" Jason asks looking on at his sword with confusion.

"I've improved it as well as given you, or whoever uses it, an 'edge' in battle," Rein tries his hardest to hold back a near escapable chuckle.

"I'm not even going to start on how bad that joke was," Sabrina says walking up behind Jason, who is now painted with the same look of confusion.

Rein, now chuckling at his own humor, explains his creation. "You see, I've serrated the blade so that there are points of entry which lead down into the blades hilt where a capsule lies. Inside the capsule is the process of mixing the blood from your enemies." Rein's talking increases as his excitement heightens. "As the blood mixes, it's then sucked up into the intravenous tube and injected into the user's blood stream."

"Hold on, slow down, Rein!" Jason says cutting Rein off. "What does the enemies blood mix with and why on earth would I want their blood inside me!?"

"That's the best part!" Rein exclaims. "The capsule is made from and engineered from my blood! So when the enemies blood is lead into the capsule, it mixes with the materials of the capsule, i.e., my blood, it makes what I like to call a 'Power Potion' and then the potion is fed inside you, granting you this power!"

"So in a sense, I'm able to use your ability to use other's abilities?" Puzzled, Jason asks for clarification.

"That's right! Pretty neat, huh?" Rein says feeling proud.

"Rein, that's genius! Now we'll really be able to take down this laboratory!"

"Honestly, I've been at it all night since I saw you training with it," Rein explains.

Jason walks over to Rein grabbing hold of the blade and placing one hand on his shoulder. "Rein, thank you. With this I think we'll be able to take down that laboratory of L's."

"Jason, I have something for you as well," Sabrina says stepping forward. Jason turns around holding his newly modified sword by his side. Sabrina takes off her shoulder strap holsters containing the 1911 SOCOMs. "Here, these are for you."

Jason grabs hold of the holster bringing it in near him staring down at the guns. He raises his head slowly as the sun rises in the horizon. "Sabrina, I've never used a gun before, I'm sorry but I don't know how much use these will be to me."

Sabrina steps toward Jason placing her hand upon his forehead. "Just wait," She whispers. Slowly, Sabrina feeds all the information from Marty's head into Jason's mind. She takes a couple of steps back waiting for Jason's mind to process all the information imported into his mind. Finally when she sees Jason understands, she whispers in a low voice, "I want you to call me Revolver from now on."

"Your father… Okay," Jason says sympathetically having never known his own father and agrees with respect "Revolver."

"Alright!" Rein shouts excitedly. "I'd say we're all ready for tomorrow!"

Jason looks back at Rein "I'd say you're right."

But are you actually ready? Jack asks Jason from within.

Honestly, I don't know, but I have no choice, Jason thinks regrettably. *I have to do this, and there's no way around it.*

Chapter Twelve

"There it is," Sabrina says putting her Jeep into park outside of the toy store. "Sinclair Toys. I don't get how she did it, but she turned one of my companies' shops into her little underground lair."

"We can ask her once we get inside," Jason says agitated. "Now, how do we get inside?"

Sabrina pulls out the blueprints to the toy shop. "It looks like there's only one point of entry and that's the front door."

"What, no windows or back doors?" Rein says sarcastically.

"No, it looks like the only entrance is through the front door," Sabrina says tracing the architect lines. "There's an elevator shaft behind the front counter leading down into the lab."

Jason looks over the blueprints laid out on Sabrina's lap. "Wait a minute. That shaft doesn't lead anywhere."

"Okay, so I didn't actually find a lab in this place, but why else would they have a shaft like that!?" Sabrina says anxiously.

"Rein, scout the place out. See if there's any other points of entry," Jason orders with angst.

"You got it," Rein replies obediently getting out of the Jeep making a sweep of the old battered building.

"Okay, so what is your reasoning for us coming to this place?" Jason says turning his attention back toward Sabrina.

"Listen, Rein said that when he was inside the lab that he saw my companies' logo right? While I was inside Osiris' head back in the cellar I got the name Jefferson out of him." Sabrina's frantically trying to justify her reasoning to Jason. "I put two and two together. This is the only place owned by my company that's on this street."

"Sabrina, he could have been thinking about Jefferson City, which is almost a thousand miles away."

"There's no way Rein could have teleported a thousand miles away from the lab and L's goons show up here attacking us."

Jason, cut her some slack, Jack says from within. *Let's at least investigate the place and see where it goes.*

Yeah, okay, Jason replies just as Rein returns.

"Alright, no windows or back doors just like she said. Only way in is through the front."

"I'll go in first," Jason says stepping out of the Jeep making his way into the toy shop. It's an old, brittle building made of wood and concrete that's falling apart. Jason turns the copper knob giving the door an ominous creaking as it slowly opens. The toy store is obviously unkept, showing signs of a lack of business. There's a man sitting at the desk, face buried in a newspaper highlighting the latest tragedy. The guy's feet are kicked up in a relaxing manner, obviously he isn't expecting anyone. "Excuse me," Jason says.

The newspaper is quickly lowered startling the man into a standing position. "Who are you? What do you want!?"

"Toy shop? Toys?" Jason says sarcastically.

"Oh, well… yeah. Get whatever you want," The man replies grumpily.

Jason walks slowly over to the desk placing both palms flat on top and leans over. In a small whisper he asks, "This isn't really a toy shop, is it?" The paper slowly lowers revealing the eyes of this so called toy salesman, his eyes flooding with red, nervous sweat. "Gotchya!" Jason punches through the paper grabbing the guy by his neck immediately slamming his face into the desk and with that, the poor guy was knocked out cold.

Jason looks around scanning the room finding a single camera above the entrance door. "Damn it," he whispers to himself. Turning back around, Jason shoves the guy off the desk taking the chair from behind and sitting so he can reach the camera up above. *Sabrina, Rein, all clear.*

"Damn, were you even sure this is the right place before putting the hurt on that guy?" Rein asks stepping inside.

"Just find the entrance. There's going to be sentries swarming this place soon," Jason says shutting the door behind Sabrina. "What do the blueprints say?"

"According to these," she says wandering behind the desk, "the entrance should be right... here."

"That's a wall," Rein comments.

"Obviously."

Jason walks over to the wall. "What if...," he says cocking back his arm. "We just make an entrance?" Then he let's loose with an adrenaline filled fist blasting a hole revealing a shaft inside.

"That works too, I guess," Sabrina says looking back down at her blueprints.

"Guys, you know there's a button here under the desk, right?" Rein says giving a click. The parts of the wall that weren't shattered to pieces retract lighting up the shaft behind. "And I'm pretty sure that's an elevator." Both Jason and Sabrina remain silent in mortification.
Ding goes the elevator as it begins its descent.

"Shit, the elevator is moving! Quick, everyone get in!" Jason says rushing inside the shaft, but it lowers too quickly. Rein and Sabrina both jump on top grabbing the hatch leading inside. "Wait!" Jason tells them as the hatch opens up. "There was a camera back there, and I was the only one seen. You two stay up there for now. Element of surprise and all that."

"Oh, right! Smart thinking!" Rein says giving an approval thumbs up. They close the hatch sitting patiently until the elevator comes to a stop. The doors open slowly into a dark corridor and extremely dense air. You could almost feel the tension on your skin by how thick the air felt, so much of it it was suffocating. Jason waits almost a full thirty seconds peering into the darkness, looking around, squinting his eyes before he settles on the idea that it's safe for him to step out, but the second he does, he's ambushed. A foot flies from outside the elevator knocking him against the wall.

"Surprise!" The person who delivered the kick shouts. "Didn't think I see ya again chump!"

Jason picks himself up off the ground immediately realizing that it's O that's standing in front of him. "Yeah, well, here I am!"

Sabrina, you and Rein keep going. I'm going to finish this, Jason telepathically says to Sabrina as he lunges toward Osiris.

The two take a nearby ventilation shaft inside crawling over Jason and Osiris being as quiet as possible. "Where are your friends, huh? The real pretty lass and the annoying one?" Osiris comments blocking an incoming punch from Jason.

"The annoying one!?" Rein whispers intensely grabbing hold of a cage blocking an opening. Sabrina grabs hold of his shoulders rearing him back, halting his descent.

"Just keep moving, Rein, Jason will take care of him," Sabrina urges as they keep crawling through. Moving slowly, using only their knees and elbows, they make their way deeper inside having an aerial view of the place. "You've been here before, where are we going?" Sabrina whispers behind Rein.

"You're the one with the blueprints, you tell me," Rein says with a snarky remark. "Oh wait! I recognize this!" Rein peers down seeing the old arena below them. "This is where they made me and the others fight each other." Sabrina scoots up beside him looking down. "Looks like they're actually bringing two test subjects out now," Rein says taking on the role of Captain Obvious as two people are shown entering the small white room. "Wait! I know that girl!" A girl steps into the room, her hair, blonde and short cut at the shoulders unevenly. Her skin appears almost as pale as the room around her, but her complexion looks healthy as if she were supposed to looks this way and her physique toned and athletic. With each step she takes, Rein can see that her posture is strong and in synch with the rest of her body. "Valentine?"

She walks into the room and right up to her opponent. Without hesitation, Valentine doesn't give her opponent time to act as she shoots out a forty inch bone drawing it up slicing the throat of her opponent dyeing the walls red. The lifeless body drops to the floor as a voice on an intercom comes out. "Thank you, Ms. V, that will be all." The doors whoosh open and without another word, she quietly walks out.

"Who was that Rein?" Sabrina asks terrified.

"Her name's Valentine, she's the one I talked about when I told Jason when I was locked up." Rein turns back around as much he can in a small space. "We have to get her outta here!"

"What!? You saw what she did to that person!" Sabrina says urgently. "We are not taking her!"

"She saved my life during one of these fights, trust me."

"Alright, lead the way."

Osiris ducks, dodging a quick roundhouse kick immediately thrusting his electrified fist into Jason's abs, knocking his breath out. Jason takes hold of his core taking a couple steps back. "Damn, that hurt. You've gotten stronger, haven't you?" Jason smirks.

"What the hell? The electricity alone should have knocked you out!" Osiris says puzzled.

Jason lifts his shirt revealing rubber under armor. "I came prepared, buddy!" He says also revealing rubber gauntlets under his sleeves. Jason reaches down grabbing hold of his sword, drawing it slowly. His mouth creates a smile like a crescent moon in the sky flipped on it's side. "Let's get serious, shall we?"

"Heh, alright, you asked for it." Osiris pulls his hands together in front of him grasping the air and instantly a beam of electricity shoots outward forming a blade within his hands.

That's like what he did back in the alleyway. Jason dashes forward slicing downward, but his blade is blocked by Osiris and his energy blade. As he's blocked, his sword passes through Osiris' having to react against an oncoming blade toward his head. *Jason!* Jack shoots adrenaline into Jason's body causing time to slow down giving him the chance to make a quick dodge and spring backwards. "Hey! That's not fair!"

"Love and war, my friend, love and war," Osiris scoffs with his blade being pointed directly at Jason. "Speaking of which." His blade then grows at an   exponential rate shooting itself toward Jason at a breakneck speed. With time still slowed Jason dashes sideways but his shoulder is still singed. Mid-jump Jason reaches inside his leather coat pulling out one of his 1911s firing off a couple shots before he hits the floor. Osiris, not acting quick enough, erects an electrified barrier stopping two of the bullets but the third shatters his collar bone. Osiris lets out a loud wail in pain dropping his arm almost instantaneously along with his energy sword. "I can't move my arm!" With those gun shots, the facility then goes on full alert.

"Alright, this is it!" Rein says stopping in the ventilation shaft above what appears to be a cell. "She's down below." He quickly rips off the cover dropping down into Valentine's cell. She gets up quickly, drawing out a blade made of bone assuming a defensive position. "Wait, wait, wait! It's me! It's Rein!"

Valentine opens her eyes from a squint and then squints again realizing who he is. "Rein?" She says dropping her bones, "is that you?"

"The one and only!" He says smiling from ear to ear.

"I had heard you escaped, but I didn't know you actually did!" She says hugging him. "What're you doing back here!?"

"Well, right, now I'm here to rescue you!"

"Rescue me? Rein, they're wanting to recruit me." She says stepping backwards.

"What? What do you mean?" He asks as Sabrina drops down beside him causing Valentine to assume an attack position again. "Whoa! Wait, she's with me!"

"Who is she!?" Valentine demands.

"Her name is Sabrina, she's helping me. She's... helped me." Rein says sounding remorseful. "But forget that for now, just know that she's a friend. What do you mean they're trying to recruit you?"

"They've given me the codename 'V,' and they want me to join their team of super powered freaks," Valentine says relaxing herself once more trusting Rein. "I don't really have a choice."

"No! Join us and we'll take this place down!" Rein says making a fist in front of him. "We'll take down L and destroy this place!"

"Did you say L!?" V shouts stepping forward. "She's alive!?"

Rein and Sabrina turn to each other looking puzzled and then back at V. "What do you mean?" Sabrina asks. "She's the one running this place."

"No, she would never do that!" V urges. "Her boyfriend cracked on her. He kidnapped me and brought me here and I thought he killed her too. He's the one behind on these tests and experiments!"

"Her boyfriend?" Sabrina asks. "Jason's not behind this, he's here with us taking her down."

"We have to stop him then! He's going after the wrong person!"

Jason slowly picks himself up off the ground holstering his gun and walks toward Osiris who is now on his knees gripping his shoulder for dear life. "You're not coming after me again, Osiris," Jason says raising his blade above him.

"Wait! You want to find L, right!?" Osiris pleads for his life with a small bargaining chip. "I can show you where she is!"

"I'll find her on my own," Jason says with anger in his voice after hearing her name again. "I'll cut down everyone in the place until I do!" He slowly pierces his sword into the right side of O's chest and placing the hilt's IV into his arm. "Let's see what you've done, Rein," Jason whispers to himself as the blood mixes in the hilt then flowing into Jason. This tingly feeling overcomes him causing this sensation of change inside within every cell of his body. The blood from O, mixed with Rein, then overcharged by the adrenaline inside Jason already shoots out a massive electrical surge through his arm and into his sword, frying Osiris, transforming him into dust. "Whoa! What the hell!?" Jason steps backward having never experienced anything like it. "I'm not sure how much longer I have with this power, but I've got to get moving!"

Jason darts down the corridor racing as fast as he can turning down hallway after hallway. The passages are now doused in red while an alarming sound echoes throughout the building. As he rounds a corner he finds himself faced with two people in front of him. "Halt! Don't take another step!" One of the masked foes says placing his hands outwards. Jason smirks at the remark dashing forward with both hands stretched out sending a blast of electricity knocking both of them down and as he runs past them, he sends a bullet into each of their skulls making sure they don't give chase. Around another corner is yet another enemy, but Jason doesn't stop this time, using his adrenaline, he grabs hold of their head as he's running past ripping their head from their shoulders and just tosses it aside as though he was tossing aside trash. "Damn it, I'm never going to find her at this rate!"

Jason! Where are you? Sabrina says from within his head telepathically.

Sabrina? Jason replies stopping in his tracks. *I don't know, I think I've gotten myself lost.*

Don't worry, I'll get a fix on your location, Sabrina assures him. *Okay, I've got it! Just wait there, you're not going to believe what we've found out!*

Two minutes later the three finally find Jason sitting up against a wall in a corridor with his eyes shut seemingly almost asleep. "Jason!?" Sabrina shouts causing him to spring to his feet. "What the hell are you doing!?"

"You said wait for you!" Jason says shrugging his shoulders. Upon Sabrina and the others getting closer, Jason recognizes the blonde girl with them. "Valentine!?" Jason says excitedly. "Is that you!?"

"Jason," She says contently. "They weren't lying..."

"What the hell are you doing here?" He asks pressing his curiosity.

"Wait, you two know each other!?" Sabrina asks intensely.

"Of course we know each other, this is L's best friend!" Jason then immediately thinks he's come to a revelation. "Valentine! What're you guys doing! Where's L!? And what's with this laboratory!?" Jason darts forward grabbing her by the neck as electricity surges though his hands.

"Wait, Jason! It's not what it looks like! She's not with L!" Sabrina says pushing Jason back telepathically.

"Her boyfriend kidnapped me and brought me here!" Valentine pleads as she catches her breath. "You have to believe me! I want to stop him as much as you do!"

"She's telling the truth, Jason!" Rein urges.

"Then take me to him," Jason says in a low, angered voice.

"Just follow m," V says taking point.

Corridor after corridor, the three following closely behind V with Jason holding one of his 1911s behind her, the alarm still echoing throughout the halls while the color red still soaks everything in its alert color. Ten minutes pass as they trek the passages with V. "This is taking too long," Jason says attempting to hurry her along.

"It's just up ahead," Valentine says pointing toward the end of the hallway. "And here it is." She says as they finally reach two wooden doors embroidered in gold and silver tribal markings. "He's a bit of douche bag."

"Let's go in," Jason commands.

"Not so fast, tough guy!" A voice from behind objects. They all turn around, but no one appears to be around. Soon after, they're each lifted into the air. "You're going in just like that! It would be too easy!" The voice finally manifests into form.

"Katerina!" Jason shouts, "and by the feel of things, Castiel must be nearby then."

"You, sir, are correct!" Castiel reveals himself stepping out of the douche bag doors. Without hesitation, Valentine holds out both of her hands shooting out bone spikes which rip though Castiel's body ceasing the zero gravity power as his life follows suit. Once their feet are placed firmly on the, ground, Sabrina draws her Single Action Army revolvers and empties all twelve shots into Katerina creating an artwork of blood splatter on the wall even Dexter would be proud of.

"Damn, you two are savage!" Rein says backing behind Jason.

"Let's go in," Jason says entering the wooden doors. Inside he finds a comfortable living space. A California King bed along with a sixty inch 4K television, a built-in kitchen and everything a normal home could think of, but what surprised him the most was what is tucked away in the corner of the room. He slowly walks over to the dark corner squinting and rubbing his eyes over and over again still trying to comprehend the sight in front of him. A sleeping girl lies in chains. Jason whispers "L, is that you?"

Chapter Thirteen

"Jason?" L says sliding up to her side, chains clinking against one another. "You came." Jason stands in the doorway motionless. His mind, full of determination and vision has completely faded to a void. He had no precognition of what he would do when he finally found her, but never did he think that he wouldn't do anything.

Valentine enters immediately rushing to L's side. "I never thought I would see you again!" Rein and Sabrina follow behind standing next to Jason working to comprehend their current situation.

"Valentine, I'm glad you're okay," L says with a very weak voice barely holding herself up. "Did he turn you too?"

"Yeah, after I found out that he locked you up, I confronted him, but Ezra and his goons took me away and I was left with the rest of the experiments," Valentine says grabbing L's hands. "But I'm here now, and we're getting out of this place!" She grabs L's arm readying herself to pick her up off the floor after she breaks the chains with a quick use of her abilities.

"Wait! Why are you in chains? I thought you were the one behind all this!?" Jason says stepping forward breaking his psychological paralysis.

"Jason, no..." L says shaking her head slowly "I've been a prisoner here just like the others. I had hoped you wouldn't get involved, but here you are." She looks down for a second pausing in contemplation then returns her gaze to Jason. "I'm just glad I was able to help in some way."

"Jason! Don't trust her! This has got to be some kind of trap!" Sabrina says stepping forward. "She knew we would come and she's trying to get inside your head again!"

"No! If she's lying, then that means Valentine is lying too, but she can't be!" Rein objects. "She helped me while she was locked up just like me. Valentine would have no reason to hurt us."

"It's true, I was locked up like Rein, like L and the rest of the people here."

"Then who was it!?" Sabrina protests, "Who was it that locked you up here, huh!?"

"His name is Christós" Valentine answers "and he's trying to make the ultimate human weapons."

Jason looks over at Sabrina in skepticism taking a couple steps away from her. "Sabrina?"

Sabrina stands in shock, dubious to the idea that her brother could be the one behind all this. "Explain yourself!" she shouts.

"Jason, I left you because Christós said he was going to kill you if I didn't," L begins to explain. "He wanted me for himself, but many times I refused his advances upon me."

"Christós turned out to be crazy! He said that if L didn't leave your then he would kill you." Valentine reinforces. "So L did what she had to."

"Okay, so if you did what he wanted, then why are you here in chains!?" Sabrina says scoffingly doubtful.

"That night, Jason, do you remember?" L asks, weak voiced still, "the night I saw you in the club and I was standing upon the DJ station?"

"What about it?" Jason asks agitated.

"I took off running after you." L lifts herself to her knees sliding down on them resting on her bottom, knees bent in front with her legs to her side and her feet resting behind. She places her hands on the floor between her legs supporting her sitting position looking upward at Jason with misty eyes. "I ran after you."

Jason becomes at a loss for words. Could he believe her? Was she lying? Where is the evidence? "Then where were you that night? Why didn't you stop me!?"

"The guy you saw me with up there was my designated bodyguard. We were out on an assignment, and I disobeyed," L says looking down. Her head lowered in silence for a few seconds manifesting tension in the air. This confrontation shatters everything Jason knew. She slowly brings her eyes to his eyes, cracking her voice as she says, "For you."

Jason delves into his mind, rushing through thoughts of "what ifs" and "how the hell" trying his hardest to comprehend what's going on. He goes back and forth in his head fighting himself about what to believe. Resorting to putting aside everything he knows to be true for the sake of the two years they spent together, he whispers in a low, calm, collected voice, "Tell me everything."

"Valentine introduced us," L says clearing her throat, relaxing her body. "He was a nice enough guy I became acquainted with, but as time went on, he began showing us spectacular things." Her face turns toward V sitting next to her then back toward Jason. "He showed us skills of pyromancy, levitation, teleportation and other amazing abilities you only see in fictional works." Guilt fills her voice as she confesses each word. "I never told you about him, not because I was hiding anything, but because I didn't think it would matter. Although, when he showed us these abilities, I knew I couldn't tell you about it. He wanted it to all be a secret." L scoots herself backwards leaning against the wall behind her while the sirens still screech throughout the facility and the walls still dyed in red lights.

"Get on with it!" Sabrina demands hating every word she hears knowing L to be her enemy.

L continued her story, making sure to quicken the pace knowing she had to convince Jason of her innocence as though the chains around her ankles and wrist weren't enough. Christós delighted L and Valentine with his special powers eventually offering them to his two female spectators. Of course no one would turn down an opportunity like that and just like that, Christós shared his power pellets with them. Small, square pills ingested by mouth which when reaching the insides of a person grants them supernatural abilities. The two spent much time with him experimenting with different powers and abilities, and they quickly became addicted to the power he was bestowing.

Christós, after some time has passed, took a liking to L. Who wouldn't? She was as beautiful and warm as the sunrise on a cold morning, as delightful as lavender on your pillow at night, and as caring as a mother's love. Christós desired her for himself but knew of Jason and the role he played. He advanced on her, making propositions but being denied each time. Christós got the idea in his head that he was more powerful than anyone with his power pellets and what does anyone do with power; they take what they want.

Christós tried taking L for himself one night and again she denied him. Enraged, he told her that if she didn't get Jason out of her life that he would do it for her. She knew he wasn't messing around when he vaporized one of his own employees that walked in on the commotion going on behind a closed door.

L was fearful of his power, especially since she wielded the powers herself. She didn't know how she was going to do it, or when she was going to do it, but she knew it had to happen. The weather just starting to warm up, the birds commencing their songs and the bees suckling nectar from blooming flowers, Jason decided it was time. He drove up in his two toned car, dressed as nicely as he could afford and walked straight up to her door. Outside there was excitement, anxious anticipation and a lack of patience, but what lie on the other side of the door he knocked upon was filled with dread, anxiety and despair from what was to come of the day. Jason walked up the stairs to her room where she sat in front of her mirror getting ready for him he thought. She refused his proposal to leave with him wherever he had planned to go with her, instead she broke his heart that day and in an instant his whole world was shattered.

As she waited for his reaction to her "burning the bridge" he slid his hand down the side of his pants and into his pocket pulling out a small box. Distress manifesting within his palm he reached out his trembling hand in anguish handing her the small box. She placed her small fingers atop the container looking to him for permission then at a slow pace took it from his possession and peered inside. Resting between two cushions was a small ring, size four, garnished with diamonds, and a sterling silver band. Her eyes lifted to Jason's hearing him speak, "I want you to have this," and, of course, she protested, but Jason knew he couldn't leave without making sure it was in her hands.

Jason rose to his feet and let them lead him out of her home and into the driver seat. He ignited the engine but hesitated to release the gas. He couldn't, he knew he shouldn't. He battled himself between letting her go and trying to work the situation out. Before he could come to a decision, L came out rounding the hood onto the driver side door. She opened the door seeing Jason sitting there without bringing his eyes to peer on hers. He wanted to hear her say that she didn't mean it, but as tears weld up in his eyes trickling down the side of his cheeks she patted his head, running her fingers through his hair and quietly said, "Oh Jason, you're so cute." She gave him a hug without the gesture being returned, but in doing so she placed an experimental power pellet in the drink residing next to him. Upon hearing the words leave her mouth, he brushed her aside, shut his door and allowed the gas to circulate through the car's metal veins. She had just made the decision for him and never did they see each other until that fateful night.

Christós, hearing of L running after Jason the night she saw him, and Sabrina, being angered again at her betrayal, resorted to the decision that she couldn't be trusted. Christós took her in chains to make sure she couldn't leave his luxurious office at the laboratory where he manufactured the pills, which initiated Valentine's confrontation with Christós that landed her behind bars and a participant in his human trials.

"Jason, I never wanted to leave you, but I had no choice," L says lifting herself off the wall struggling to get to her feet. "I never wanted to hurt you... I loved you and the ring you gave me that day meant the world to me!" Valentine lifted L up the rest of the way to her feet.

"L, I don't know what to say," Jason said trying to decide if he believed her or not. "What do I do?"

"I don't know the situation between you two that well, but if Valentine believes her, then I'm going to have to do the same Jason," Rein throws his two cents into a sea coins. "Only

Sabrina can really get inside her head and tell you if she's telling the truth though."

Jason and Rein turn toward Sabrina standing a few feet away, her face turning red with anger that Jason would even consider believing L. Her jealousy was overcoming her entire body creating much animosity. "She's lying! She's a lying little bitch!" She yelled out without hesitation. L's legs gave out on her, causing her body to collapse. Without thinking or initiation, adrenaline surged through Jason's veins pumping in his legs, and he quickly dashed to L catching her just in time. He lowered himself to his knees holding her in his arms. "Jason!" Sabrina shouted surprised.

"I'm sorry, L!" Jason said pulling her tight into his body "I'm sorry I ever doubted you!"

"Jason," L began. "I'm sorry it took me so long." She continued, "Jason, drink up please."

"What?" Jason asked. The walls were no longer covered in red lights. The lights were turned on appearing as bright as the sun.

"Drink this, Jason," L said again holding a cup to his lips. Jason brought his head back from her seeing a small, white, styrofoam cup filled with clear water. Jason blinked and the walls became so bright they presented a pure white form. "Drink this, Jason."

Jason reached his hand up grabbing the cup becoming astonished by the chains around his wrist. "What the hell!?" Jason exclaimed in fear. He turned around to look at Sabrina who stood at the back of the room, yet she no longer had her Single Action Army Revolvers at her waist nor did she have on her leather, half cut jacket. Instead of jeans she wore white slacks with a white shirt to match. "Sabrina?"

"Do as she says, Jason." Sabrina says calmly.

Jason, confused and scared, lifted the cup up to his mouth and drank. Upon swallowing the liquid he saw Christós standing behind L in a white lab coat with his hands folded behind his back. "He's stabilizing, Doctor," Sabrina said; Christós thanked her in response.

"Christós?" Jason asked then turned his attention back to L. "L? What's going on?"

L got up and walked Jason over to a nearby couch sitting down and placing his head on her lap with his body sprawled out on the rest of the furniture. Christós took the chair adjacent placing it in front of L and Jason placing himself in it with Sabrina taking to his side standing politely. "Six months ago you were in a car accident," Christós begins. "Many people died. You, however, survived and Sabrina here was the paramedic on sight," he said motioning to her by his side. "She found you trapped in your very badly smashed car; legs jammed between the steering wheel and the windshield."

"No, that's how I found her," Jason protested, "I used my strength to rip the door off and snap the steering wheel."

"No, Jason," L said, "they used the jaws of life to pull you out of the car." Jason didn't respond, he just lay there in L's lap reveling in the feeling of being so close to her. His mind was going crazy with all the thoughts of trying to comprehend. It may have been the drug he was just administered or the substance L was providing with her presence, but his body was completely still and calm void of anxiety or distress.

"This is the first time we've been able to get through to you," Sabrina says, still beside Christós. "You've been trapped inside a delusional state of mind creating a scenario of fiction since being admitted here."

Jason turned looking up at L with hope, "You and I are still together?"

L's eyes filled with tears, her heart sank into her stomach with the shakes rustling in her hands trying to hold onto Jason, "No, I still left you that night." Her head shakes left and right dropping tears onto his face. "I just couldn't bring myself to come see you all this time."

"Jason, I'm not sure if you can fathom this, but I believe the reason we've finally gotten through to you is because of this girl here," Christós says with confidence. "But now it's time for her to go." Christós stands up cueing L to do the same, lifting Jason's head off her lap.

"Don't go!" Jason pleads.

"I'm sorry, Jason," L says as Dr. Christós and Nurse Sabrina walk out. L takes Jason in her embrace holding him tightly. "I'll get you out soon, Jason." She leans closer to his ear whispering very softly, "I love you." Letting go, she turns and walks out as the padded door closed encasing him in his white cell. He peers through the barred window placed in the door and watches as she walks away.

Christós walks beside L leading her out and Jason hears the last utterance before they disappear around the corner. "Thank you for visiting him. We'll take care of him here at Sinclair Institution."

www.ingramcontent.com/pod-product-compliance
Lightning Source LLC
Chambersburg PA
CBHW051419280526
45785CB00003B/1084